T0210997

Lecture Notes in Computer Science　　10222

Commenced Publication in 1973
Founding and Former Series Editors:
Gerhard Goos, Juris Hartmanis, and Jan van Leeuwen

Editorial Board

More information about this series at http://www.springer.com/series/7411

Alain Pirovano · Marion Berbineau
Alexey Vinel · Christophe Guerber
Damien Roque · Jaizki Mendizabal
Hervé Bonneville · Hasnaâ Aniss
Bertrand Ducourthial (Eds.)

Communication Technologies for Vehicles

12th International Workshop
Nets4Cars/Nets4Trains/Nets4Aircraft 2017
Toulouse, France, May 4–5, 2017
Proceedings

 Springer

Editors
Alain Pirovano
ENAC
Toulouse
France

Marion Berbineau
IFSTTAR
Villeneuve d'Ascq
France

Alexey Vinel
Halmstad University
Halmstad
Sweden

Christophe Guerber
ENAC
Toulouse
France

Damien Roque
ISAE-SUPAERO
Toulouse
France

Jaizki Mendizabal
Ceit-IK4
Asociación Centro Tecnológico
Donostia-San Sebastian
Spain

Hervé Bonneville
Mitsubishi Electric R&D Centre Europe
Rennes
France

Hasnaâ Aniss
IFSTTAR
Versailles
France

Bertrand Ducourthial
Université de Technologie de Compiègne
Compiègne
France

ISSN 0302-9743   ISSN 1611-3349 (electronic)
Lecture Notes in Computer Science
ISBN 978-3-319-56879-9   ISBN 978-3-319-56880-5 (eBook)
DOI 10.1007/978-3-319-56880-5

Library of Congress Control Number: 2017937145

LNCS Sublibrary: SL5 – Computer Communication Networks and Telecommunications

Printed on acid-free paper

This Springer imprint is published by Springer Nature
The registered company is Springer International Publishing AG
The registered company address is: Gewerbestrasse 11, 6330 Cham, Switzerland

Preface

The Communication Technologies for Vehicles Workshop series provides an international forum on the latest technologies and research in the field of intra- and inter-vehicles communications. It is organized annually to present original research results in all areas related to physical layer, communication protocols and standards, mobility and traffic models, experimental and field operational testing, and performance analysis among others.

First launched by Tsutomu Tsuboi, Alexey Vinel, and Fei Liu in Saint Petersburg, Russia (2009), the Nets4Workshops series (Nets4Cars/Nets4Trains/Nets4Aircraft) have been held in Newcastleupon-Tyne, UK (2010), Oberpfaffenhofen, Germany (2011), Vilnius, Lithuania (2012), Villeneuve d'Ascq, France (2013), Offenburg, Germany (2014 Spring), Saint Petersburg, Russia (2014 Fall), Sousse, Tunisia (2015 Spring), Munich, Germany (2015 Fall), San Sebastian, Spain (2016 Spring), and Halmstad, Sweden (2016 Fall).

These proceedings contain the papers presented at the 12th International Workshop on Communication Technologies for Vehicles Nets4Workshops series (Nets4Cars/ Nets4Trains/Nets4Aircraft 2017), which took place in Toulouse, France, in May 2017, organized by ENAC (French Civil Aviation University) with the technical support of IFSTTAR, France, and Halmstad University, Sweden.

The call for papers resulted in 16 submissions. Each of them was assigned to the international Technical Program Committee to be reviewed at least by two independent reviewers. The co-chairs of the three Technical Program Committees (Nets4Cars, Nets4Trains, and Nets4Aircraft) selected 12 full papers for publication in these proceedings and presentation at the workshop, four of them for Nets4Cars, seven for Nets4Trains, and four for Nets4Aircraft. In addition, two demonstration papers were also accepted. The order of the papers presented in these proceedings was aligned with the workshop program.

The general co-chairs and the Technical Program Committee co-chairs extend a sincere "thank you" to all the authors who submitted the results of their recent research as well as to all the members of the hard-working comprehensive Technical Program Committee that worked on the reviews.

March 2017

Alain Pirovano
Marion Berbineau
Alexey Vinel
Jaizki Mendizabal
Hervé Bonneville
Bertrand Ducourthial
Hasnaâ Aniss
Damien Roque
Christophe Guerber

Organization

General Co-chairs

Alain Pirovano	ENAC (French Civil Aviation University), France
Berbineau Marion	IFSTTAR, France
Vinel Alexey	Halmstad University, Sweden

TPC Co-chairs (Nets4Trains)

Jaizki Mendizabal	CEIT and Tecnun (University of Navarra), Spain
Herve Bonneville	Mitsubishi Electric, France

TPC Co-chairs (Nets4Aircraft)

Damien Roques	ISAE-SUPAERO, France
Christophe Guerber	ENAC (French Civil Aviation University), France

TPC Co-chairs (Nets4Cars)

Bertrand Ducourthial	Université de Technologie de Compiegne, France
Hasnaâ Aniss	IFSTTAR, France

Steering Committee

Alexey Vinel	Halmstad University, Sweden
Marion Berbineau	IFSTTAR, France
Jaizki Mendizabal	CEIT and Tecnun (University of Navarra), Spain
Alain Pirovano	ENAC, France
Mickaël Royer	ENAC, France
Nicolas Larrieu	ENAC, France
Fabien Garcia	ENAC, France

Technical Program Committee

Alexey Vinel	Halmstad University, Sweden
Marion Berbineau	IFSTTAR, France
Emilie Masson	IFSTTAR, France
Divitha Seetharamdoo	IFSTTAR, France
Alain Pirovano	ENAC, France
Christophe Guerber	ENAC, France
Guthemberg Da Silva Silvestre	ENAC, France

Fabien Garcia	ENAC, France
Nicolas Larrieu	ENAC, France
Jean-Aimé Maxa	ENAC, France
Quentin Vey	ENAC, France
Mickaël Royer	ENAC, France
Alexandre Chabory	ENAC, France
Christophe Morlaas	ENAC, France
Gentian Jakllari	ENSEEIHT, France
Bertrand Ducourthial	Université de Technologie de Compiegne, France
Damien Roques	ISAE-SUPAERO, France
Albert Abello	ISAE-SUPAERO, France
Cyrille Siclet	GIPSA-Lab, France
Laurent Ros	GIPSA-Lab, France
Arriola Aitor	Ikerlan, Spain
Pierre Siohan	IRISA, France
Jean-Baptiste Doré	CEA Leti, France

Hosting Institution

ENAC (French Civil Aviation University), Toulouse, France

Organizing Committee

Alain Pirovano	ENAC, France
Mickaël Royer	ENAC, France
Nicolas Larrieu	ENAC, France
Fabien Garcia	ENAC, France
Quentin Vey	ENAC, France
Hélène Weiss	ENAC, France

Co-organizer and Sponsor Institutions

CEIT, Spain
IFSTTAR, France
Halmstad University, Sweden

Contents

Nets4Aircraft and UAV

Performance Assessment of a New Routing Protocol in AANET

Quentin Vey[1,3]([⊠]), Alain Pirovano[1,3], Stéphane Puechmorel[2,3], and José Radzik[4]

[1] ENAC, TELECOM/Resco, Toulouse, France
{vey,pirovano}@recherche.enac.fr
[2] ENAC, MAIAA, Toulouse, France
puechmorel@recherche.enac.fr
[3] Univ de Toulouse, Toulouse, France
[4] Université de Toulouse/ISAE,
10 avenue Édouard Belin, BP 54032, Toulouse, France
radzik@isae.fr

Abstract. Routing is a critical issue in mobile ad hoc networks. The routing algorithm must take into account the specific properties of the network such as its topology, the mobility of the nodes and their number. In this paper, we present a simulation-based study of the performances of our innovative routing protocol named NoDe-TBR (Node Density TBR) that takes into account the actual node density distribution. The considered ad hoc network is an Aeronautical Ad hoc NETwork (AANET), a future communication system enabling air↔air and air↔ground communications beyond the radio range of the sender. This context and the communication architecture have been modeled in a realistic way based on replayed aircraft trajectories, a realistic access layer, and application that should be deployed in the future.

Keywords: MANET · AANET · Ad hoc · Trajectory-based routing · NoDe-TBR

1 Introduction

An Aeronautical Ad hoc NETwork (AANET) is an ad hoc network in which inflight aircraft can act as senders, receivers and relays for digital data transmissions. They are studied as a complement to traditional aeronautical communication systems such as satellite or cellular systems [1].

The feasibility of an AANET for air-ground communications over the North Atlantic Tracks (NATs) has already been demonstrated in previous studies [2], and several routing algorithm have been proposed. Amongst them, we have proposed Node Density TBR (NoDe-TBR), an innovative and promising solution. As described in [3], it presents better performances in terms of reachability and delay than classical routing algorithms for a fraction of the signalization traffic volume.

© Springer International Publishing AG 2017
A. Pirovano et al. (Eds.): Nets4Cars/Nets4Trains/Nets4Aircraft 2017, LNCS 10222, pp. 3–14, 2017.
DOI: 10.1007/978-3-319-56880-5_1

In this paper, we present an assessment NoDe-TBR with two types of applications proposed by civil aviation authorities. This assessment has been conducted by simulation in a realistic environment, with replayed aircraft trajectories and realistic access layers. A periodic transmission of several parameters of the Flight Data Recorders (FDR) is used in the first experiment. The associated data traffic consists only in air→ground transmissions. A set of relevant air traffic control applications have been simulated in the second experiment. These latter generate a data traffic in both directions between aircraft and ground stations.

The rest of the paper is organized as follow: Section 2 describes NoDe-TBR. The settings used in the simulations are described in Sect. 3. The experiment with the FDR application and the experiment with the air traffic control applications are described and analyzed respectively in Sects. 4 and 5. Finally, our conclusions are given in Sect. 6

2   NoDe-TBR

NoDe-TBR is a trajectory-based routing protocol proposed and described in details in [3]. We present here a short description of its main features.

2.1   TBR

NoDe-TBR is based on the concept of Trajectory-Based Routing (TBR) [4]. In TBR, a geographic trajectory (geopath) is computed by the sender. The full geopath that a packet has to follow is carried in its header (source routing), and the relays forwards it on a route matching this geopath (see Fig. 1). It can be seen as an evolution of cartesian routing, where the forwarding is based only on the position of the destination.

A TBR routing protocol has two independent parts:

– A geopath computation algorithm;
– A forwarding algorithm.

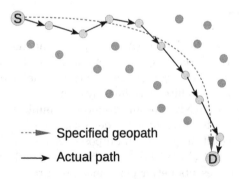

Fig. 1. General principle of TBR.

The geopath computation algorithm must take into account the properties of the network (node movement, geographic distribution of the nodes...). The forwarding algorithm is used to select the next hop amongst the neighbors each time a packet is forwarded.

2.2 Geopath Computation

In NoDe-TBR, the geopath design is based on two assumptions. First, the higher the aircraft density along the geopath is, the higher the delivery probability will be. Second, the shorter the geopath is, the higher the delivery probability will be. Hence the geopath computation method used in NoDe-TBR takes into account the local aircraft density as well as geographical length of the geopath.

In the rest of the paper, d denotes the aircraft density. It can be computed with a kernel density estimation [3] (an example of such density map is shown in Fig. 2).

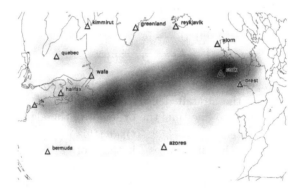

Fig. 2. Aircraft density map (greyscale: dark = high density).

Definition. From the previous assumptions, it can be concluded that the geopath should minimize a quantity of the form $\frac{l}{d}$ with l the length of the geopath, and d the aircraft density (the aircraft density is a function of the position). The geopath between a sender S and a destination D is defined as a function $\gamma : [0; 1] \rightarrow \mathbb{R}^2$ such that:

– $\gamma(0) =$ Position of S
– $\gamma(1) =$ Position of D
– γ minimizes the integral (1)

$$\int_0^1 \|\gamma_i'(t)\| \cdot i(\gamma(t))dt \tag{1}$$

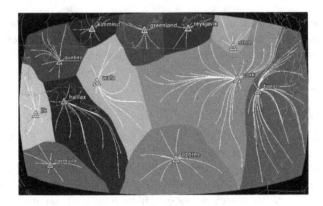

Fig. 3. Examples of geopaths toward ground stations and associated Voronoi map.

Consequently, γ is a minimizing geodesic between S and D. i is an "index" function used to take into account the aircraft density. In NoDe-TBR, we have:

$$i : \left| \begin{array}{l} [0;1] \longrightarrow \mathbb{R} \\ t \longmapsto \frac{1}{D+d(\gamma(t))^\alpha} \end{array} \right. \tag{2}$$

In (2), D is the average aircraft density over the whole map, and $d : \mathbb{R}^2 \to \mathbb{R}$ is the function associating the aircraft density to each point of the map. α is an exponent that can be used to fine-tune the behavior of the algorithm.

The length of γ is given by $l = \int_0^1 \|\gamma_i'(t)\|dt$ (this is (1) without the index function). The trajectory that minimizes l is the shortest path between S and D. The index function i changes this behavior: the function γ that minimizes (1) is "attracted" by high density areas because i is lower in these areas.

Computation. The geopaths are computed in three steps:

1. The Fast Marching Method (FMM) [5] is used to compute the front propagation time. The seed of the FMM is set to the position of the sender.
2. The minimizing geodesic between the positions of the destination and the sender is then computed with a gradient descent algorithm. This step produces a geopath in the form of a sequence of geographical coordinates (represented in white in Fig. 3).
3. The number of coordinates of the geopath is reduced with the Ramer-Douglas-Peucker algorithm [6].

Update. Because the spatial aircraft density changes during the day and from day to day, the aircraft density estimation and the geopaths must be regularly updated.

2.3   Routing Protocol

Forwarding Method. Several forwarding method have been assessed in [3], and ADR (Advance Delay Ratio) provides the best performances. This method has been selected for NoDe-TBR. In order to learn the positions of its neighbors (needed to select the next hop), each aircraft uses an Automatic Dependent Surveillance - Broadcast (ADS-B) in/out transceiver. This device broadcasts the position of the aircraft and receives the positions of its neighbors. This equipment is being mandated for airliners.

Signalization Traffic. The NoDe-TBR routing protocol exploits the geopath computation method previously defined in order to forward packets in the network. Because this method involves the use of a density map, signalization data must be exchanged between aircraft so that every aircraft can build a density map.

NoDe-TBR makes use of a positioning system (such as GPS) in order to learn its current position. Airliners are already equipped with such systems.

It remains however necessary to exchange data between aircraft in order to make them aware of the position of the other aircraft that are beyond the radio range. In NoDe-TBR, each aircraft broadcasts periodically an estimation of its future trajectory. These broadcasts are done via a flooding dissemination mechanism to ensure that every node in the network receives the trajectory predictions.

In NoDe-TBR, a periodic refresh policy is used. The refresh interval is set 20 min, approximatively the time required by an aircraft to travel half the radio range while flying at its cruise speed. It has to be noted that one node can compute geopaths toward every other node in the network with the same density map. One can thus consider that the signalization traffic generation is a proactive process in NoDe-TBR.

3   Performance Assessment Settings

3.1   Realistic Access Layer Model

In order to realistically model the point to point communications, we use a modified version of the RP-CDMA protocol. The original RP-CDMA is described in [7] and its performances with classical routing algorithms are studied in [8].

Description of RP-CDMA. RP-CDMA is a protocol which solves the problem of code attribution inherent to CDMA access layer. The payload of a RP-CDMA frame is spread with a randomly selected code, and an identifier for this code is included in the header of the frame (cf. Fig. 4).

This frame structure provides a separation between the signalization channel (headers) and the data channels (payload). If the set of payload codes is large enough, RP-CDMA is mainly limited by header collisions.

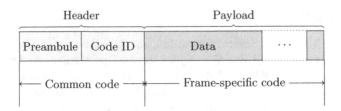

Fig. 4. Base structure of a RP-CDMA frame.

In order to improve RP-CDMA performances in long-range ad-hoc networks, two modifications have been made to the original protocol. First, an aggregation policy has been implemented in order to increase the size of the payload and reduce the header to payload ratio. Thus the load on the signalization channel is reduced, and the frame losses are reduced. Secondly, p-persistent CSMA is used as access method.

The different parameters that define the behavior of RP-CDMA have been optimized with the method described in [8], and in the same conditions as in this paper. In particular, the optimal maximum frame length is 9000 bits.

Modelisation Assumptions. The RP-CDMA model uses the following conservative assumptions:

- If two headers collide, then both frames are considered unrecoverable.
- If there are less than $maxPayload_{rx} - 1$ other frame colliding simultaneously with a given payload, this payload can be decoded. Otherwise, it is not recoverable [9].
- If the distance between a sender and a receiver is above a given range, the frame is not taken into account.

As demonstrated in [2], a radio range of 350 Km is enough to have an average connectivity over 90% in the North Atlantic flight corridor. Based on this publication and the results in [9], we use the following values: $maxPayload_{rx} = 25$, $range = 350$ km and $bitrate = 800$ kb/s.

The length of the RP-CDMA frame header is set to 80 bits. The size of the fixed information control fields is 136 bits, and 46 bits are added for each encapsulated packet. The access layer modules uses FIFO queues to store a maximum of 100 pending packets.

3.2 Simulation Environment

The models are developed and implemented in the simulator OMNeT++ [10]. We use the UDP and IP model from the INET framework [11]. We use custom modules for the traffic generation, the node mobility, the access layers and the routing.

3.3   Node Positions

In this paper, we focus on the North Atlantic Tracks (NAT) [1] because they cover an area where it is impossible to deploy a ground-based communication system. We replay real aircraft position data from Eurocontrol historical traffic repository [12] in order to take into account the diversity of constraints that are applied to aircraft trajectories. Several different days are replayed to add statistic diversity.

Because of the computational cost of the simulation, we have to restrict the simulations to three sets of replayed trajectories, each of them consisting in a one-hour time slot for three different days. The average Instantaneous Aircraft Count (IAC) for each set of trajectories is represented in Table 1.

Table 1. Average IAC for each set of trajectories.

Aircraft load	Average IAC
Low	102
Medium	315
High	567

In order to match the different possible air routes and hence maximize the probability of delivery, twelve ground stations (represented as black triangles on Fig. 2) are placed on land masses around the area of interest.

3.4   Metrics

In order to quantify the performances of the AANET, the following metrics are defined.

Normalized Reachability. We define reachability as the ability to send packets bidirectionally between an aircraft and a ground station (it is similar to a *ping availability*).

In an AANET topology, some nodes may not be able to reach a ground station because they are too far from any other nodes, independently of the performance of the routing algorithm. In order to use a metric without this bias, the reachability values are normalized by the "connectivity to the ground". Let $G = (A \cup S, E)$ be the graph representing our network. The vertices in A are the inflight aircraft and those in S are the ground stations. The edges E are the feasible links. Let N_p be the number of aircraft in A for which a path to a ground station exists. The "connectivity to the ground" is defined as $C = \frac{N_p}{|A|}$.

The *normalized reachability* is then defined as $\frac{R}{C}$, with R the ratio of reachable aircraft.

E2E Delay. The end to end (E2E) delay is measured for each received data packet.

E2E AR. The End to End Acknowledged Ratio (E2E AR) is computed from the end-to-end application-level acknowledgements. This metric takes only into account the data messages that are sent while the aircraft is reachable (see previous definition).

P2P AR. The Point to Point Acknowledged Ratio (P2P AR) measures the ratio of packets that are acknowledged over one-hop transmissions.

4   Flight Data Recorder Application

The first application assessed here consists in the transmission of a part of the flight data that are currently only stored in Flight Data Recorders (FDR). It has been notably proposed in [13] after the loss of the flight AF447, for which the wreckage could not be easily located. It would allow the analysis of some flight parameters even if the FDRs can not be recovered.

4.1   Generated Data Traffic

The data traffic generated to model this application consist in UDP datagrams sent toward ground stations. These datagrams are acknowledged by the ground station. These acknowledgements (or the lack thereof) are used by the sender aircraft to detect whether a ground station is reachable.

We simulate three sizes of application messages described in [13]: 9 bytes, 96 bytes and 1536 bytes. One datagram is sent every second.

4.2   Results

The results of this experiment are presented in Figs. 5, 6 and 7. In every graph in this paper the 95% confidence interval are represented by black vertical error bars.

The graph Fig. 5 represents the normalized reachability. We observe two trends, one for the two lowest sizes of data messages, the other for data messages of 1536 bytes. The same segregation can be observed in Fig. 6. Figure 7 displays however similar results for every size of messages.

4.3   Discussion

The fact that the normalized reachability does not reach 100% can be explained by the fact that the computation method used to generate the geopath does not

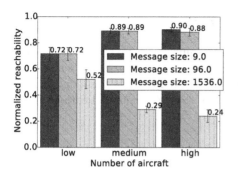

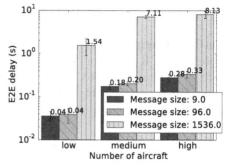

Fig. 5. Normalized reachability (FDR)   **Fig. 6.** E2E delay (FDR)

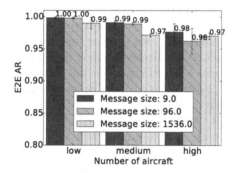

Fig. 7. E2E AR (FDR)

guarantee that a path between the sender and the destination exists. Because the probability of finding a relay along the geopath increases with the number of aircraft, the scenarios with the lowest number of aircraft are more heavily impacted.

The difference in terms of reachability and E2E delay observed for the biggest size of messages (1536 bytes = 12288 bits) is explained by the fact that the data message size is larger than the optimal payload size for the layer 2 (9000 bits). Consequently, its performances are worse for the biggest packets. This problem can be solved by implementing packet fragmentation based on a Maximum Transmission Unit (MTU) to 9000 bits.

In every scenario, the E2E AR is high (over 96%). Consequently, the reachability can be used as an effective metric to determine if the AANET can be used to transmit data to a ground station. If an aircraft detects that it is not reachable, it can decide to use an alternative communication system.

In most cases, the performances of our communication system based on AANET are promising for this FDR application: the normalized reachability is around 90% and the average E2E delay is below 200 ms.

5   COCR Air-Ground Applications

The Communications Operating Concept and Requirements for the Future Radio System (COCR [14]) is a document produced by Eurocontrol which defines air traffic control applications. These applications, based on digital communications systems, will complement and partially replace the voice communications that are currently used for air traffic control.

5.1   Generated Data Traffic

The data traffic generated in this experiment reproduces the unicast applications defined for the Oceanic Remote Polar (ORP) areas in [14]. It consists in UDP packets, whose sizes and periods of sending are set according to [14]. We use the values specified for the phase 2 of digital communication deployment. In this phase, the digital communications become the primary mean for air-ground communications. This phase is expected to start in 2020.

In our model, a simple acknowledgement and retransmission mechanism is implemented in the application layer: if no acknowledgement is received after 3 s, then the message is retransmitted.

In order to reduce the load around the ground stations, the ground station application module generate data toward a given aircraft only when the latter is reachable. This behavior prevents the transmission of packets that could anyway not reach their destination and removes an unnecessary load from the network. To that end, the air→ground application traffic doubles as a network probe traffic in order to let a ground station know which aircraft may be reached. In particular, the application called "SURV" in [14] sends a packet towards the ground every five seconds, which ensures that enough air→ground traffic is generated for that purpose.

5.2   Results

The simulations results are presented in Figs. 8, 9 and 10. For the scenario with a low aircraft load, the performances considering the three metrics are similar to the previous experiment. The normalized reachability and the E2E delay of the other scenarios are worse than in the previous experiment.

The P2P AR ratio is represented in Fig. 11.

5.3   Discussion

Because in this experiment ground stations receive and send data traffic (unlike in the FDR experiment), the radio channel is more loaded in their vicinity than in the rest of the network.

The consequence of this concentration of traffic is illustrated in Fig. 11. For the scenarios "medium number of aircraft" and "high number of aircraft", there is a clear difference in the P2P AR measured at the ground stations and in the

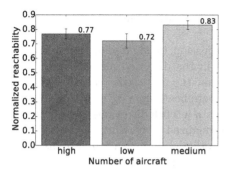

Fig. 8. Normalized reachability (COCR)

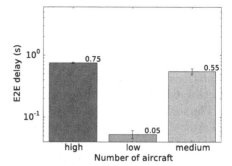

Fig. 9. E2E delay (COCR)

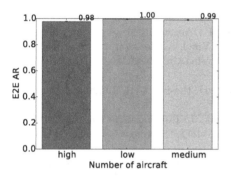

Fig. 10. E2E AR (COCR)

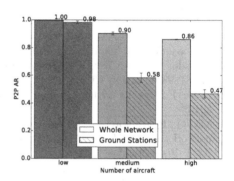

Fig. 11. P2P AR (COCR)

whole network. The scenario "low number of aircraft" displays a P2P AR very close to 1, which shows that the ground stations are far less loaded than in the other scenarios.

The load of the access layers in the scenarios "medium number of aircraft" and "high number of aircraft" explains that the normalized reachability and delay are worse than in the FDR experiment. There are no significant differences for the "low number of aircraft" scenario because the ground stations are not overloaded.

In every scenario, the E2E AR is high (over 98%). As consequence, we can consider that it is also relevant to use this metric in the context of COCR applications in order to determine whether the AANET can be used to reach a ground station.

6   Conclusions

In this paper, we have presented an innovative routing algorithm for AANETs: NoDe-TBR. The performances of this algorithm have been assessed in realistic conditions: on replayed trajectories and with a realistic access layer model.

Two sets of applications proposed by the civil aviation authorities have been simulated.

The first one consist in a remote transmission of flight data parameters, for which the data traffic is only generated in the direction air→ground. The simulations results are promising and show that the proposed architecture is an effective data communication system for this application.

The second set of applications generates data in both directions (air→ground and ground→air). In this experiment, the normalized reachability is above 70%. It means that, when used in complement to other communication systems, the AANET can handle the majority of the aircraft in the NAT.

References

1. Vey, Q., Pirovano, A., Radzik, J., Garcia, F.: Aeronautical ad hoc network for civil aviation. In: Sikora, A., Berbineau, M., Vinel, A., Jonsson, M., Pirovano, A., Aguado, M. (eds.) Nets4Cars/Nets4Trains/Nets4Aircraft 2014. LNCS, vol. 8435, pp. 81–93. Springer, Cham (2014)
2. Besse, F.: reseaux ad hoc aeronautiques. Ph.D. thesis, ISAE, Toulouse, February 2013
3. Vey, Q., Puechmorel, S., Pirovano, A., Radzik, J.: Routing in aeronautical ad-hoc networks. In: 2016 IEEE/AIAA 35th Digital Avionics Systems Conference (DASC), pp. 1–10, September 2016
4. Niculescu, D., Nath, B.: Trajectory based forwarding and its applications. In: Proceedings of the 9th Annual International Conference on Mobile Computing and Networking, MobiCom 2003, pp. 260–272. ACM, New York (2003)
5. Sethian, J.A.: A fast marching level set method for monotonically advancing fronts. Proc. Natl. Acad. Sci. **93**(4), 1591–1595 (1995)
6. Ramer, U.: An iterative procedure for the polygonal approximation of plane curves. Comput. Graph. Image Process. **1**(3), 244–256 (1972)
7. Mortimer, T., Harms, J.: A MAC protocol for multihop RP-CDMA ad hoc wireless networks. In: 2012 IEEE International Conference on Communications (ICC), pp. 424–429, June 2012
8. Vey, Q., Pirovano, A., Radzik, J.: Performance analysis of routing algorithms in AANET with realistic access layer. In: Mendizabal, J., et al. (eds.) Nets4Cars/Nets4Trains/Nets4Aircraft 2016. LNCS, vol. 9669, pp. 175–186. Springer, Cham (2016). doi:10.1007/978-3-319-38921-9_18
9. Kempter.: Modeling and evaluation of throughput, stability and coverage of RP-CDMA in wireless networks. Ph.D. thesis, University of Utah (2006)
10. OMNeT++ (2013). http://www.omnetpp.org
11. INET (2014). http://inet.omnetpp.org
12. Eurocontrol: Data demand repository, vol. 2, September 2015. http://www.eurocontrol.int/ddr
13. BEA. Flight data recovery working group report. Technical, Bureau d'Enquétes et d'Analyses pour la sécurité de l'aviation civile, December 2009
14. Eurocontrol and the Federal Aviation Administration (FAA). COCR: Communications operating concept and requirements for the future radio system - version 2.0 (2006)

Miniaturized Antennas for Vehicular Communication Systems

Alexandre Chabory[(✉)], Christophe Morlaas, and Bernard Souny

ENAC, TELECOM-EMA, 31055 Toulouse, France
alexandre.chabory@recherche.enac.fr

Abstract. This paper contains an overview on 3 antennas, whose properties are of interest for vehicular communications. The first one is a wide-band miniaturised antenna with a stable radiation pattern. The second one is a low-profile antenna inspired by high impedance surfaces. The last one is a helical-ring antenna, whose radiation is toward a half-space in circular polarisation without the use of a metallic reflector. For all of them, the basic principles and simulation results are presented. For the last one, a prototype is also analysed.

Keywords: Antenna · Miniaturisation · Wide-band

1 Introduction

In vehicular applications, antennas operate under several constraints. These constraints may concern RF properties, such as the bandwidth, the polarisation, and the radiation pattern. They may also concern the size, the shape and the weight. For example, for small vehicles as UAVs, the weight, the thickness and the presence of a ground plane, whose size is typically significant in terms of wavelength, are key-difficulties.

In this article, an overview on three antennas is presented in the context of vehicular applications. All of them are miniaturised antennas, i.e. they are small with respect to the wavelength. The first one is a wide-band antenna with a frequency-independent omni-directional radiation pattern [1]. The second one is thin and inspired from metamaterials [2]. The last one presents a half-space radiation in circular polarisation without using any metallic reflector or ground plane [3,4].

This article is organised as follows. For each antenna, the principles are explained and simulation results are presented. For the third antenna, a prototype is also studied both from simulation and measurement results.

2 Wide-Band Miniaturised Antenna with a Stable Radiation Pattern

2.1 Principle

To obtain a quasi omnidirectional radiation pattern for a wide frequency band, a disk-loaded folded monopole can be used [5,6]. Nevertheless, this solution yields

© Springer International Publishing AG 2017
A. Pirovano et al. (Eds.): Nets4Cars/Nets4Trains/Nets4Aircraft 2017, LNCS 10222, pp. 15–20, 2017.
DOI: 10.1007/978-3-319-56880-5_2

a radiation pattern that is not stable over frequency, i.e. significant variations in the pattern appear in the upper part of the frequency band. An alternative solution is presented here [1]. Its structure allows to maintain the radiation pattern in the upper part of the frequency band. The antenna, presented in Fig. 1, comprises an upper disk, a smaller lower disk, six straight wires connecting both disks, and six helical wires connecting the upper disk to the ground plane. The feeding is realised on a wire located between the lower disk and the ground plane.

The radiation of this antenna corresponds to the combination of two modes: an unfolded-monopole mode and a transmission-line mode, both of which are equivalent to resonant circuits. The first mode is associated with the following elements of the antenna structure: the upper disk, the 6 straight wires and the lower disk. The second mode is associated with the upper disk and the helical-wire cage.

Taking into account both modes, a resonant circuit model can be found to determine the central frequency and bandwidth in terms of impedance matching. The analysis of the current on this antenna shows that to improve the radiation pattern stability over a large band-width, the number and the length of the helical and straight wires must be increased.

2.2   Simulation Results

In this section, the antenna of Fig. 1 is simulated using Feko. The dimensions of the structure are as follows. The upper and lower disks are of diameter 12 cm and 7 cm, respectively. Their distances to the ground plane are 5.5 cm and 1.5 cm. The wire diameter is 2 mm. The helix rotation is a quarter of a turn.

The simulation result gives a frequency band for this antenna going from 511 MHz to 1074 MHz, i.e. approximately one octave. In Fig. 2, the antenna gain pattern is displayed in the horizontal plane. As desired, the pattern remains omni-directionnal in all the frequency band.

Fig. 1. Disk-loaded monopole with a 6-wires helical cage

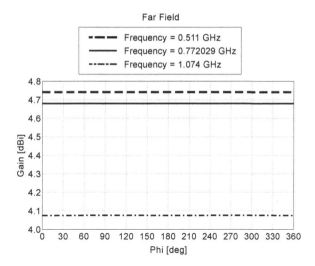

Fig. 2. Gain (dBi) in the horizontal plane of the disk-loaded monopole with a 6-wires helical cage

3   Thin Antenna Inspired by High Impedance Surfaces

3.1   Principle

For other types of applications in vehicular communications, the antenna thickness must be small. A way to realise low profile antennas is to use high-impedance surfaces (HIS). Indeed, any electric source placed parallel and close to such a surface has an optimal radiation. HIS are generally designed from periodic surfaces (metamaterials) for which the reflection coefficient is $\Gamma = +1$. In the design phase, the surface is generally assumed to have an infinite number of periodic cells so as to use Bloch-Floquet theory. In practical applications, only a small number of cells are however used due to size constraints.

In the limiting case, this yields a procedure to design thin antennas from a given basic structure [2]. Firstly, the basic structure is periodized, i.e. considered to be one cell of an infinitely periodic surface. Then, by simulation, the periodized structure is optimized so as to behave as a HIS. Finally, only two or three cells are used to obtain the antenna.

An example of application of this method is illustrated in Fig. 3. The basic structure is a rectangular metallic plate placed on top of a ground plane. The periodization method is firstly applied. Then, only two cells are kept.

3.2   Simulation Results

The final size of the rectangular plate is 67 mm × 55 mm. The gap between the two plates is 1 mm. The plates are 6 mm above the ground plane. For such dimensions, the antenna has 100 MHz of bandwidth centered at 1.575 GHz. In Fig. 4, the radiation pattern of this antenna is displayed.

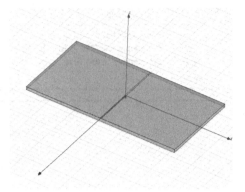

Fig. 3. HIS inspired antenna

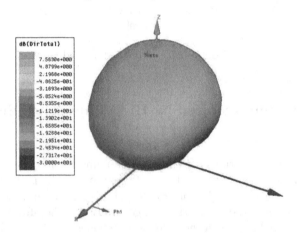

Fig. 4. Directivity pattern (dBi) of the HIS inspired antenna

4 Helical-Ring Antenna

4.1 Principle

With both previous antennas, the presence of a metallic ground-plane is assumed. For small vehicular applications as UAVs, this ground plane is an issue because of its weight and size. An antenna whose radiation is oriented toward a half-space without any large planar metallic structure would therefore be of interest. Besides, for numerous communication applications, e.g. SatCom, circular polarisation is also desirable. Theoretically, a half-space radiation in circular polarisation can be achieved by combining 2 elementary electric dipoles and 2 elementary magnetic dipoles. Two of the dipoles can be obtained from a straight helix antenna [7,8]. Thus, to combine the four dipoles, two straight helices must be used. This can be done relying on a helical ring structure [3,4] as illustrated in Fig. 5. The direction of the circular polarisation is defined by the handedness

Fig. 5. Helical ring

of the helix. Note also that the direction of the radiation can be electrically switched frontward or backward by modifying the feeding.

4.2   Example of Application

In Fig. 6, a prototype of helical ring is presented. The helix has 4 turns. The right-handed helical ring has an outer diameter of 38 mm, an inner of diameter 5.5 mm, and height of 13 mm. The antenna is fed so that the radiation is directed upward.

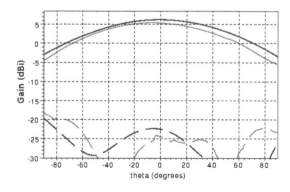

Fig. 6. Picture of the prototype

Fig. 7. Helical ring gain pattern (dBi): RHCP measurement (red line), RHCP simulation (blue line), LHCP measurement (dashed red line), LHCP simulation (dashed blue line). (Color figure online)

Both in simulations and measurements, the antenna central frequency is of 1.575 GHz with a 2:1 VSWR bandwidth of 21 MHz. In Fig. 7, the measured and simulated radiation patterns are compared in the upper half-space. The matching between simulation and measurement is acceptable. Besides, the purity of the right-hand circular polarisation (RHCP) is very good for any elevation angle.

5　Conclusion

In this article, three antennas have been presented. They offer properties that may be useful for vehicular communications. The first one combines a reduced size and a radiation pattern which remains the same regardless of the frequency. The second one is low profile. The last one radiates toward a half-space in circular polarisation without using any metallic reflector.

References

1. Morlaas, C., Souny, B., Chabory, A.: Cage-shaped wideband antenna based on folded monopoles. In: International Symposium on Antennas and Propagation (ISAP), Taipei, Taiwan, December 2014
2. Morlaas, C., Souny, B., Chabory, A.: Slot planar antenna on metallic support with large bandwidth. In: European Conference on Antennas and Propagation (EuCAP), Rome, Italy, April 2011
3. Souny, B.: Antenne autodirectrice en polarization circulaire - self-directing antenna with circular polarization (2010)
4. Morlaas, C., Souny, B., Chabory, A.: Helical-ring antenna for hemispherical radiation in circular polarization. IEEE Trans. Antennas Propag. **63**(11), 4693–4701 (2015)
5. Seeley, E.: An experimental study of the disk-loaded folded monopole. IRE Trans. Antennas Propag. **4**(1), 27–28 (1956)
6. Goubau, G.: Multi-element monopole antennas. In: Proceedings of ECOM-ARO Workshop on Electrically Small Antennas, pp. 63–67 (1976)
7. Wheeler, H.A.: A helical antenna for circular polarization. Proc. IRE **35**(12), 1484–1488 (1947)
8. Kraus, J.D.: The helical antenna. Proc. IRE **37**(3), 263–272 (1949)

Improving Spectral Efficiency While Reducing PAPR Using Faster-Than-Nyquist Multicarrier Signaling

Cyrille Siclet[1,2], Damien Roque[3(✉)], Alexandre Marquet[1,2], and Laurent Ros[1,2]

[1] Univ. Grenoble Alpes, GIPSA-Lab, 38000 Grenoble, France
{cyrille.siclet,alexandre.marquet,laurent.ros}@gipsa-lab.fr
[2] CNRS, GIPSA-Lab, 38000 Grenoble, France
[3] Institut Supérieur de l'Aéronautique et de l'Espace (ISAE-SUPAERO),
Université de Toulouse, 31055 Toulouse, France
damien.roque@isae-supaero.fr

Abstract. Multicarrier modulations are widely used in mobile radio applications due to their adaptability to the time-frequency characteristics of the channel, thus enabling low-complexity equalization. However, their intrinsically high peak-to-average power ratio (PAPR) is a major drawback with regard to implementation issues (*e.g.*, power amplification efficiency, regulatory constraints...).

In this paper, we confirm that the PAPR can be decreased as the signaling density (*i.e.*, spectral efficiency at fixed constellation size) increases, even in the case where symbols cannot be perfectly reconstructed using a linear system. In such a two-dimensional generalization of faster-than-Nyquist (FTN) systems, PAPR distribution models from the literature are confirmed by simulation results. Furthermore, for a fixed number of subcarriers, we show that a sufficient condition to yield the optimal PAPR distribution at the output of a critically sampled transmitter is to specify pulse shapes as tight frames. Finally, simulations are performed in the more realistic case of an oversampled transmitted signal.

Keywords: Multicarrier modulations · Faster-Than-Nyquist signaling · Peak-to-average power ratio · Power amplification

1 Introduction: PAPR of Faster-than-Nyquist Multicarrier Modulations

Vehicular communications often imply radio propagation in a mobile multipath environment (*e.g.*, car-to-car communications, miniature unmanned aerial vehicles, etc.). Input-output relation of such a propagation channel usually accounts for time and frequency selectivity [5,10,18]. In this context, multicarrier modulations can be specified as an approximate eigenstructure of the channel by allocating information symbols to coordinates in the time-frequency plane as

© Springer International Publishing AG 2017
A. Pirovano et al. (Eds.): Nets4Cars/Nets4Trains/Nets4Aircraft 2017, LNCS 10222, pp. 21–32, 2017.
DOI: 10.1007/978-3-319-56880-5_3

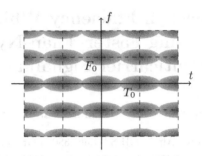

Fig. 1. Representation of a multicarrier signal with a rectangular lattice in the time-frequency plane using Gaussian pulse shapes.

illustrated in Fig. 1 [7,8]. A careful design of the multicarrier system (*i.e.*, time-frequency lattice, pulse shapes, etc.) can significantly lower equalization's computational complexity compared to more specific waveforms (*e.g.*, single carrier modulations, cyclic-prefixed orthogonal frequency-division multiplexing) [13].

With an increasing need of spectral efficiency, the "faster-than-Nyquist" (FTN) signaling technique has been extended to multicarrier modulations [14]. Denoting F_0 the inter-carrier spacing and T_0 the multicarrier symbol duration, the system is referred to as FTN when its density $\rho = 1/(F_0 T_0)$ is strictly greater than one. Such a constraint implies that transmitted information symbols cannot be perfectly reconstructed using a linear receiver. In other words, for a finite bandwidth and a fixed information symbol constellation of size N_c, any increase of spectral efficiency $\eta = \rho \log_2(N_c)$ beyond $\log_2(N_c)$ comes at the cost of inter-pulse interference that should be mitigated with the help of non-linear receivers [9,15].

Any transmitted multicarrier signal results from a sum of many independent information symbols shaped and modulated onto subchannels of equal bandwidth. It is thus characterized by an intrinsically high peak-to-average power ratio (PAPR) [6]. Since the peak power is usually limited either by regulatory or integration constraints (*e.g.*, linear power amplification), the average power should be adjusted consequently, thus penalizing the link budget.

In this paper, we show that PAPR decreases as the density increases, even in the FTN context ($\rho > 1$), provided that appropriate pulse shapes are used. To this extent, we refer to statistical PAPR models initially assessed for $\rho \leq 1$ [1,19]. We show that a sufficient condition to yield an optimal PAPR distribution with a critically sampled FTN multicarrier transmitted signal is to specify pulse shapes as tight frames. Simulations also reveal the need of more accurate PAPR models in the context of oversampled systems.

The paper is organized as follows. Section 2 presents the multicarrier transmitted signal model considering any density and pulse shape. Section 3 defines PAPR and recalls statistical models from the literature while generating empirical distributions through simulations. The FTN case is extensively investigated in order to emphasize the influence of $\rho > 1$ combined with several practical pulse shapes sampled at the Nyquist rate or above. Finally, conclusion and insights are given in Sect. 4.

2 System Model: (Non)-rectangularly Shaped Multicarrier (FTN) Modulations

Let $K > 0$ be the number of multicarrier symbols to be transmitted, and $M > 0$ be the number of subcarriers. We define $\{c_{m,n}\}_{(m,n)\in I} \in C^{M \times K}$, $I = \{0,\ldots,M-1\} \times \{0,\ldots,K-1\}$ the sequence of zero-mean, independent and identically distributed (i.i.d) information symbols, usually taken in a finite set (or constellation). In the continuous-time domain, the transmitted multicarrier signal is obtained by shaping each symbol by a time-frequency shifted version of a prototype (or pulse shape) $g(t) \in R$ [17]:

$$s(t) = \sum_{(m,n)\in I} c_{m,n} g_{m,n}(t), \quad t \in R \tag{1}$$

with

$$g_{m,n}(t) = g(t - nT_0)e^{j2\pi mF_0 t}. \tag{2}$$

In practical applications, M and K are bounded, $\{c_{m,n}\}_{(m,n)\in I}$ is square summable and $g(t)$ is also square integrable such that the sum in (1) converges. One recalls that $F_0 > 0$ and $T_0 > 0$ represent elementary symbol spacing, in frequency and time, respectively. By defining the transmission density as $\rho = 1/(F_0 T_0)$, it can be shown that a necessary condition to perfectly recover the symbols $c_{m,n}$ without interpulse interference (IPI) using a linear receiver is $\rho \leq 1$ [3, Chap. 9]. Consequently, such a density parameter can be used to generalize the single carrier Nyquist criterion[1] to the two-dimensional case (*i.e.*, time-frequency) such that three cases arise [16]:

- $\rho < 1$ (or equivalently, $T_0 > 1/F_0$) corresponds to a *slower-than-Nyquist* (STN) or undercritical system;
- $\rho = 1$ (or equivalently, $T_0 = 1/F_0$) corresponds to a Nyquist rate or critical system;
- $\rho > 1$ (or equivalently, $T_0 < 1/F_0$) corresponds to a *faster-than-Nyquist* (FTN) or overcritical system.

Over an additive white Gaussian noise (AWGN) channel, when $\rho \leq 1$, symbols are linearly recovered without IPI and with maximization of the signal-to-noise ratio (SNR) when $\{g_{m,n}(t)\}_{(m,n)\in I}$ constitutes an orthonormal family, *i.e.*:

$$\langle g_{m,n}, g_{p,q} \rangle = \int_{-\infty}^{+\infty} g^*_{m,n}(t) g_{p,q}(t) \, \mathrm{d}t = \delta_{m,p} \delta_{n,q} \tag{3}$$

---

[1] The Nyquist criterion mentioned herein refers to the interference free condition, as initially stated in [11] in the case of single carrier transmission.

with δ the Kronecker delta and $(m, n, p, q) \in \boldsymbol{I}^2$. On the contrary, when $\rho > 1, \{g_{m,n}(t)\}_{(m,n)\in \boldsymbol{I}}$ cannot be an orthogonal family and IPI cannot be removed by a linear receiver, but the signal-to-interference-plus-noise ratio (SINR) is maximized when $\{g_{m,n}(t)\}_{(m,n)\in \boldsymbol{I}}$ forms a tight frame [16]. What is more, according to the Wexler–Raz theorem [3, p. 214], this is equivalent to say that $\tilde{g}_{m,n}(t)$ forms an orthonormal family sharing the same prototype in the dual time-frequency lattice:

$$\tilde{g}_{m,n}(t) = \sqrt{F_0 T_0} g(t - n/F_0) e^{j2\pi mt/T_0}. \tag{4}$$

For numerical purposes, the system may also be described at discrete-time. The transmission generator $g(t)$ is supposed to have a bandwidth W_g. It results an overall system bandwidth $W = (M-1)F_0 + W_g$ that can be approximated by MF_0 hereafter assuming $|W_g - F_0|/(MF_0) \ll 1$. In practice, it is generally the case if we consider a large number of subcarriers. As a consequence, the signal can be sampled at critical rate $1/T_s = MF_0$ and we denote N the number of samples per multicarrier symbol such that $T_0 = NT_s$. Note that the density can be rewritten as $\rho = M/N$ and considering a unique multicarrier symbol, the FTN case is illustrated in the discrete-time domain by a number of samples per multicarrier symbol N less than the number of subcarriers M.

Assuming that $g(t)$ has most of its energy in $[-T_s/2; L_g T_s - T_s/2[$, the discrete-time transmission prototype can be expressed as

$$g[k] = \begin{cases} \sqrt{T_s} g(kT_s) & \text{if } k \in \{0, \ldots, L_g - 1\} \\ 0 & \text{otherwise.} \end{cases} \tag{5}$$

where the factor $\sqrt{T_s}$ is used for energy normalization. From (1), the discrete-time transmitted signal can be expressed as

$$s[k] = \sqrt{T_s} s(kT_s) = \sum_{(m,n)\in \boldsymbol{I}} c_{m,n} g_{m,n}[k], \tag{6}$$

with

$$g_{m,n}[k] = \sqrt{T_s} g_{m,n}(kT_s) = g[k - nN] e^{j2\pi \frac{m}{M} k}. \tag{7}$$

A complete reception stage (including iterative decoding or decision feedback equalization techniques) may be found in [9] and shows that FTN systems may allow an almost perfect recovery of the symbols at an extra computational cost compared to orthogonal linear systems. Such receiving structures won't be detailed hereafter since we focus on the PAPR issue, which only involves the transmitted signal model given in (1) and (6).

3   Benefits of FTN Multicarrier Signaling on PAPR

The PAPR of a signal is defined as the ratio of its peak power and its average power. For a continuous-time multicarrier transmitted signal as defined in (1), assumed with a finite time support $[0; T]$ with $T \geq T_0$, we have:

$$\text{PAPR} = \frac{\max_{t \in [0,T]} |s(t)|^2}{\mathbb{E}\{\frac{1}{T} \int_0^T |s(t)|^2 \, dt\}} \tag{8}$$

where $\mathbb{E}\{\cdot\}$ is the expectation operator. For a discrete-time (critically sampled) signal as defined in (6), we denote $N_t = T/T_s$ and we obtain the following expression:

$$\text{PAPR}_\text{d} = \frac{\max_{k \in \{0,...,N_t-1)\}} |s[k]|^2}{\mathbb{E}\{\frac{1}{N_t} \sum_{k=0}^{N_t-1} |s[k]|^2\}} \tag{9}$$

Note that $s[k]$ in the previous relation can be interpolated by a factor N_i. It is consequently clear that PAPR_d approaches PAPR as N_i becomes large ($N_i = 4$ is typically sufficient). As discussed in [19], the maximization in (8) or (9) is often performed over a multicarrier symbol duration.

It may be derived from [19] that if

1. $c_{m,n}$ symbols are zero-mean and i.i.d.,
2. $g(t)$ is time-limited,
3. $\sum_{n \in \mathbf{Z}} |g(t - nT_0)|^2 > 0$ for all $t \in \mathbf{R}$,
4. $s[k]$ samples are independent from each other,

then, for M large enough (typically, $M \geq 8$), the complementary cumulative distribution function (CCDF) of the discrete-time PAPR may be approximated thanks to the formula:

$$\Pr\{\text{PAPR}_\text{d} > \gamma\} \approx 1 - \prod_{k=0}^{N-1} \left(1 - e^{-\gamma x[k]}\right) \tag{10}$$

with

$$x[k] = \frac{\|g\|^2}{N \sum_{n \in \mathbf{Z}} |g[k - nN]|^2} \tag{11}$$

and, what is more, the best PAPR performance is achieved when $x[k] = 1$, so that we then get

$$\Pr\{\text{PAPR}_\text{d} > \gamma\} \approx 1 - \left(1 - e^{-\gamma}\right)^N . \tag{12}$$

Note that the former expression matches traditional (rectangularly shaped) OFDM waveform when $N = M$ (i.e., in the absence of cyclic prefix). Nevertheless, if we manage to satisfy conditions 1 to 4 with an FTN multicarrier system, this PAPR performance will be improved since $\rho > 1$ implies $N < M$. Conditions 1 and 2 may obviously be imposed regardless of the system's density. We will now show that conditions 3 and 4 are also satisfied if we use tight frames, as recommended in [16] for the sake of SINR maximization.

Indeed, if $g_{m,n}(t)$ (or $g_{m,n}[k]$ for the discrete-time equivalent system), is a tight frame, then the dual family $\tilde{g}_{m,n}(t) = \sqrt{F_0 T_0} g(t - n/F_0) \exp(j2\pi mt/T_0)$ forms an orthonormal family. This also means that $g(t)$ satisfies the Nyquist criterion at rate F_0:

$$\sum_{m \in \mathbf{Z}} |\hat{g}(f - mF_0)|^2 = \text{cst}, \tag{13}$$

with $\hat{g}(f)$ the Fourier transform of $g(t)$.

According to [2], (13) implies that the power spectral density of $s[k]$ is white if $c_{m,n}$ are i.i.d and assuming a critical sampling frequency, namely $1/T_s = MF_0$. What is more, using the central limit theorem as in [1,19], we get that samples $s[k]$ follow a Gaussian distribution and should be considered as independent within our transmitted signal model (6). What is more, the fact that $g_{m,n}(t)$ forms a tight frame also implies that [3, p. 210]

$$\sum_{n \in \mathbf{Z}} |g(t - nT_0)|^2 = T_0 \, \|g\|^2 \tag{14}$$

so that $\sum_{n \in \mathbf{Z}} |g[k - nN]|^2 = N \, \|g\|^2$, and $x[k]$ defined in (11) is therefore equal to 1.

These results are confirmed by simulations in which we use several prototypes of tight frames: the first one maximizes the time-frequency localization (denoted as TFL) [12], the second one is a square root raised cosine with roll-off equal to $\rho - 1$ (denoted as SRRC) and the third one is a rectangular pulse-shape of length M (denoted as RECT-M) or N (denoted as RECT-N). Even if the M-samples rectangular window (RECT-M) does not generate a tight frame, it may be shown that the samples of the subsequent multicarrier samples signal are also independent. Nevertheless, in this case, the corresponding $x[k]$ is not a constant, leading to a degraded PAPR performance.

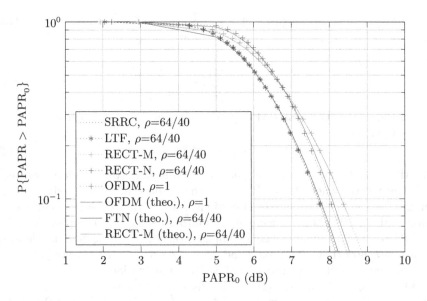

Fig. 2. Discrete-time PAPR comparison for $M = 64$, a quadrature phase shift keying (QPSK) constellation, $\rho = 1.6$, and various prototypes.

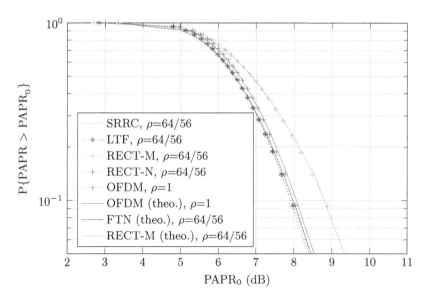

Fig. 3. Discrete-time PAPR comparison for $M = 64$, a quadrature phase shift keying (QPSK) constellation, $\rho \approx 1.14$, and various prototypes.

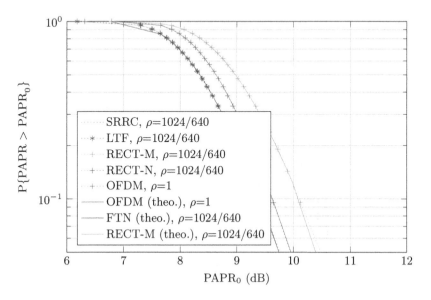

Fig. 4. Discrete-time PAPR comparison for $M = 1024$, a quadrature phase shift keying (QPSK) constellation, $\rho = 1.6$, and various prototypes.

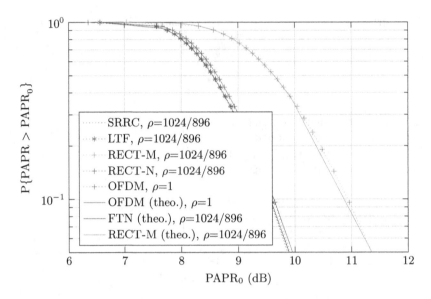

Fig. 5. Discrete-time PAPR comparison for $M = 1024$, a quadrature phase shift keying (QPSK) constellation, $\rho \approx 1.14$, and various prototypes.

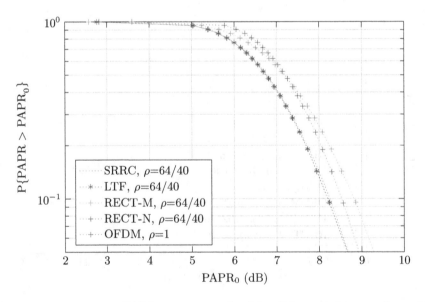

Fig. 6. Continuous-time PAPR comparison for $M = 64$, a quadrature phase shift keying (QPSK) constellation, $\rho = 1.6$, and various prototypes.

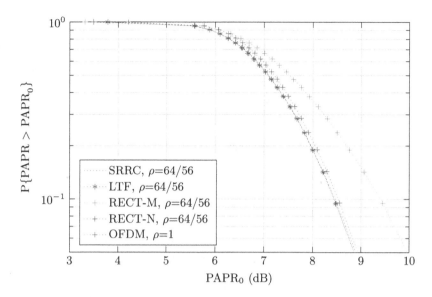

Fig. 7. Continuous-time PAPR comparison for $M = 64$, a quadrature phase shift keying (QPSK) constellation, $\rho \approx 1.14$, and various prototypes.

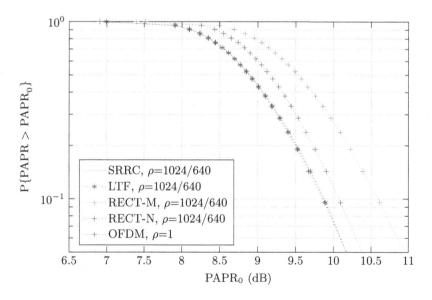

Fig. 8. Continuous-time PAPR comparison for $M = 1024$, a quadrature phase shift keying (QPSK) constellation, $\rho = 1.6$, and various prototypes.

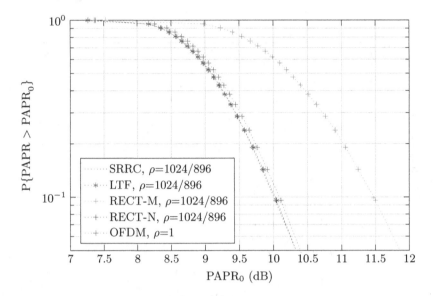

Fig. 9. Continuous-time PAPR comparison for $M = 1024$, a quadrature phase shift keying (QPSK) constellation, $\rho \approx 1.14$, and various prototypes.

As for the CCDF of the PAPR, we first compare it in the discrete-time case with the theoretical formula given by (12). Figures 2, 3, 4, and 5 show a very good match with the theoretical formula whereas the use of a non-tight frame (RECT-M) gives a discrete-time PAPR distribution very different. These simulations also confirm that increasing the number of subcarriers improves accuracy (*i.e.*, the relevance of the central limit theorem).

We then compare the continuous-time PAPR distribution ($N_i = 4$) obtained for the same systems. In this case, the theoretical formula does not hold since signal samples may not be considered independent anymore. Nevertheless, Figs. 6, 7, 8, and 9 show that the relative positions of the different curves are unchanged. Thus, this also confirms that increasing ρ not only increases the spectral efficiency, but also improves the PAPR. In fact, for a given number M of subcarriers, the distribution of the PAPR is the same as the one of an orthogonal system using $M/\rho \leq M$ subcarriers.

4   Conclusion

In this article, we have firstly shown that PAPR distribution as derived in [19] remains accurate in the case of practical critically sampled FTN multicarrier systems. Furthermore, optimum PAPR performance can be obtained in the FTN case provided that (i) pulse shapes are chosen as tight frames and (ii) a sufficiently large number of subcarriers is considered. Interestingly, at a given number of subcarriers, FTN multicarrier systems based on tight frames achieve better PAPR performance than traditional OFDM.

An open issue concerns the case where the multicarrier signal samples are not independent. Hypothesis of independence is clearly not relevant when dealing with an oversampled transmitted multicarrier signal. Consequently, the PAPR distribution model derived in [1,19] does not hold anymore. As future work, one could investigate the conditions under which the transmitted samples are independent. A second step could involve the derivation of more general PAPR models (or instantaneous transmitted power [4]) allowing to confirm (or revoke) the constraints to be fulfilled by optimum pulse shapes.

References

1. Chafii, M., Palicot, J., Gribonval, R.: Closed-form approximations of the peak-to-average power ratio distribution for multi-carrier modulation and their applications. EURASIP J. Adv. Signal Process. **2014**(1), 121 (2014). http://dx.doi.org/10.1186/1687-6180-2014-121

2. Chongburee, W.: Analysis of power spectral density of digitally-modulated combined pulse trains. In: Annual Conference on Electrical Engineering/Electronics Computer Telecommunication and Information Technology (ECTI) (2005)

3. Christensen, O.: Frames and Bases: An Introductory Course. Birkhauser, Boston (2008)

4. Ciochina, C., Buda, F., Sari, H.: An analysis of OFDM peak power reduction techniques for wimax systems. In: International Conference on Communication (ICC), vol. 10, pp. 4676–4681. IEEE, June 2006

5. Haas, E.: Aeronautical channel modeling. IEEE Trans. Veh. Technol. **51**(2), 254–264 (2002)

6. Han, S.H., Lee, J.H.: An overview of peak-to-average power ratio reduction techniques for multicarrier transmission. IEEE Wirel. Commun. **12**(2), 56–65 (2005)

7. Jung, P.: Pulse shaping, localization and the approximate eigenstructure of LTV channels (special paper). In: Wireless Communication and Networking Conference (WCNC 2008), pp. 1114–1119. IEEE (2008)

8. Kozek, W., Molisch, A.F.: Nonorthogonal pulseshapes for multicarrier communications in doubly dispersive channels. IEEE J. Sel. Areas Commun. **16**(8), 1579–1589 (1998)

9. Marquet, A., Siclet, C., Roque, D.: Analysis of the faster-than-Nyquist optimal linear multicarrier system. Comptes Rendus Physique, February 2017

10. Matolak, D.W.: Channel modeling for vehicle-to-vehicle communications. IEEE Commun. Mag. **46**(5), 76–83 (2008)

11. Nyquist, H.: Certain topics in telegraph transmission theory. Trans. Am. Inst. Electr. Eng. **47**(2), 617–644 (1928)

12. Pinchon, D., Siohan, P.: Closed-form expressions of optimal short PR FMT prototype filters. In: Global Telecommunication Conference (GLOBECOM), pp. 1–5. IEEE, December 2011

13. Roque, D., Siclet, C.: Performances of weighted cyclic prefix OFDM with low-complexity equalization. IEEE Commun. Lett. **17**(3), 439–442 (2013)

14. Rusek, F., Anderson, J.: The two dimensional Mazo limit. In: International Symposium on Information Theory (ISIT), pp. 970–974. IEEE, September 2005

15. Rusek, F., Anderson, J.: Multistream faster than Nyquist signaling. IEEE Trans. Commun. **57**(5), 1329–1340 (2009)

16. Siclet, C., Roque, D., Shu, H., Siohan, P.: On the study of faster-than-Nyquist multicarrier signaling based on frame theory. In: International Symposium on Wireless Communication Systems (ISWCS), pp. 251–255. IEEE, August 2014
17. Siclet, C., Siohan, P., Pinchon, D.: Oversampled orthogonal and biorthogonal multicarrier modulations with perfect reconstruction. In: International Conference on Digital Signal Processing, vol. 2, pp. 647–650. IEEE (2002)
18. Sklar, B.: Rayleigh fading channels in mobile digital communication systems. I. characterization. IEEE Commun. Mag. **35**(9), 136–146 (1997)
19. Skrzypczak, A., Siohan, P., Javaudin, J.P.: Analysis of the peak-to-average power ratio of the oversampled OFDM. In: International Conference on Acoustics Speech and Signal Process. (ICASSP). vol. 4, p. IV. IEEE, May 2006

An SDR Based Embedded Channel Sounder

Hervé Boeglen[1(✉)], Albekaye Traore[1,2], and Manuel Milla Peinado[1,3]

[1] University of Poitiers, XLIM Lab, UMR CNRS 7252, Poitiers, France
herve.boeglen@univ-poitiers.fr
[2] Airbus Group, 1, Rond-Point Maurice Bellonte, 31707 Blagnac Cedex, France
[3] ISL, 5, Rue du Général Cassagnou, 68300 Saint-Louis, France

Abstract. This demonstration is about a low cost SDR based channel sounder. It is built around a low power embedded system embedded on a flying drone and uses OFDM technology to sound a wireless channel in time and frequency. After treatment, the data recovered at the receiver station allows for a complete channel characterization that leads to channel models which can then be used in digital communication simulators.

Keywords: Channel sounding · Software Defined Radio (SDR) · OFDM

1 Using OFDM for Channel Sounding

In a classical OFDM system using coherent digital modulation, it is necessary to have a mean of estimating the phase shifts induced by the channel. This is generally done by using pilots added to the data [1]. In the case of our channel sounder, we use only pilots. This leads to a channel sounding system that samples the wireless channel accurately in time and frequency. Figure 1 shows an example of the channel frequency response H(f,t) obtained by using this method. Thanks to an IFFT operation on the frequency response, one can get the channel impulse response (CIR) h(τ,t). This is the main idea of our channel sounding system. In the following section, we describe the implementation details.

2 The SDR Based Channel Sounder

Figure 2 shows that the channel sounder is built around two Software Defined Radio (SDR) equipment [2]. It relies on a packet mode transmission. The number of OFDM subcarriers used by the packet can vary from 64 to 2048 when the transmission bandwidth varies from 10 MHz to 50 MHz. These elements are adjusted according to the type of channel to be measured. The data carried by the subcarriers is a pseudo random QPSK sequence optimized in order to reduce the peak amplitude power ratio (PAPR) which is a known issue with OFDM. Basically, the emitter transmits continuously OFDM packets (with variable size and inter-packet interval). At the receiver side, the packets are received in their complex form and recorded in a file for later treatment. After applying classical OFDM synchronization algorithms, and for each OFDM packet,

© Springer International Publishing AG 2017
A. Pirovano et al. (Eds.): Nets4Cars/Nets4Trains/Nets4Aircraft 2017, LNCS 10222, pp. 33–37, 2017.
DOI: 10.1007/978-3-319-56880-5_4

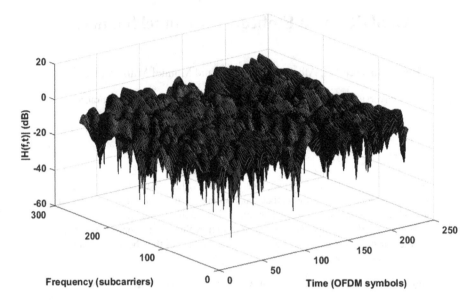

Fig. 1. OFDM channel sounding example

two main pieces of information are available, namely the channel transfer function H(f,t) (after an FFT operation) and the channel impulse response h(τ,t) (CIR, after an IFFT operation). Hence, the channel can be tracked over time by monitoring the evolution of this information over the transmitted packets.

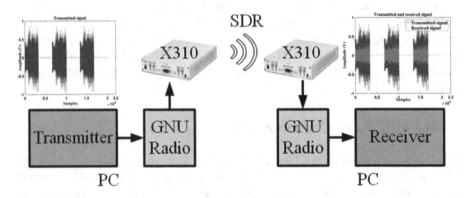

Fig. 2. OFDM channel sounder components

Although the sounder can be operated with laptops, there are a number of situations when it is not possible to use the full feature sounder presented before. We have therefore designed a small size and weight factor and battery powered solution. This has been possible thanks to the usage of the SoC FPGA technology which combines, in the same chip, a low power microprocessor tailored for embedded applications (low power) and an FPGA which allows to design high speed digital interfaces to wideband RF front ends

[3]. The result is a system, weighting only 450 g and achieving a maximal transmission rate of 50 MSps. Table 1 summarizes the main features of this system and Fig. 3 shows a picture of the system embedded on an hexacopter drone.

Table 1. Embedded SDR channel sounder characteristics

Carrier frequency	70 MHz to 6 GHz
Transmit power	Up to +18 dBm
Data rate	Up to 50 MSps transmit rate
Power	2200 mAh 3S LiPo battery
Autonomy	1 h 30 mn

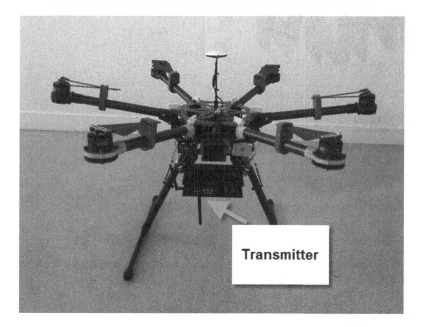

Fig. 3. An hexacopter drone equipped with the channel sounder

3   System Validation and Results

In order to validate the OFDM channel sounder we have characterized several indoor and outdoor environments using two other tools that can be considered as references since they have been validated by previous research works. The first tool is a 3D ray tracing software called RaPSor and developed in our lab [4]. The second tool is a vector network analyzer (VNA) which is a classical measurement equipment used for indoor channel sounding.

We use a dedicated Matlab user interface (UI) to extract the measured parameters. Figure 4 shows an example of the evolution of the channel transfer function H(f,t) and channel impulse response h(τ,t) over 120 OFDM symbols for an outdoor channel using the drone of Fig. 3.

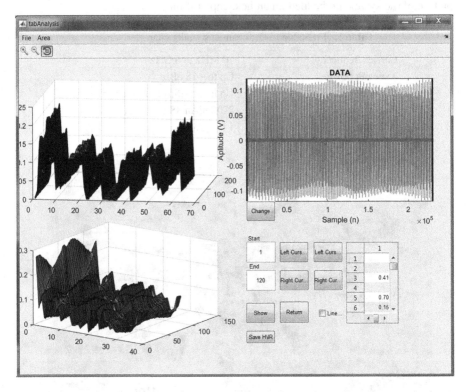

Fig. 4. Evolution of the channel transfer function H(f,t) and channel impulse response h(τ,t) over 120 OFDM symbols

4   Conclusion

We have presented an OFDM based channel sounding technique that can be implemented thanks to relatively low cost SDR equipment. It can also be integrated on a small low power embedded system using the SoC-FPGA technology. The information gathered from the channel consists in the frequency response and the CIR. Hence, the technique allows for the identification of the main multipath components (MPCs) of a wireless environment, as would a VNA do. The embedded system with the drone will be presented at the 12th International workshop on communication technologies for Vehicles in Toulouse the 4th and 5th May 2017.

References

1. Canet, M.-J., et al.: FPGA implementation of an OFDM-based WLAN receiver. Microprocess. Microsyst. **36**(3), 232–244 (2012). Elsevier

2. https://www.ettus.com/product/details/X310-KIT
3. https://www.altera.com/products/soc/overview.html
4. Escarieu, F., et al.: Outdoor and indoor channel characterization by a 3D simulation software. In: Proceedings of the 12th International Symposium on Personal, Indoor and Mobile Radio Communications (PIMRC 2001), Boston, Mass, USA, pp. B105–B111, October 2001

Nets4Trains

A Multimedia Streaming System for Urban Rail Environments

Justas Poderys[1(✉)], Jahanzeb Farooq[1,2], and Jose Soler[1]

[1] Technical University of Denmark, Kongens Lyngby, Denmark
{juspo,jafar,joss}@fotonik.dtu.dk
[2] Siemens A/S, Ballerup, Denmark
jahanzeb.farooq@siemens.com

Abstract. Due to a large number of mostly stationary users inside a train and the availability of a radio connection to the outside world, urban rail environments serve as promising candidates for multimedia distribution systems deployment. This work proposes to offload the individual per-passenger cellular network connections by using the excessive Communications-Based Train Control (CBTC) radio link bandwidth to deliver multimedia streams to a train, where it is subsequently distributed to the passengers using peer-to-peer based data distribution. Connections among the train passengers are implemented using the Wi-Fi Direct connectivity and data exchange is coordinated by using the Peer-to-Peer Streaming Peer Protocol. This work presents the solution and evaluates it in the scope of urban rail deployment. Network emulation tests are used to analyze the factors impacting the number of concurrent users that can use the proposed system. This work also proposes future work lines that can be used to improve the system's design.

Keywords: Wi-Fi direct · Peer-to-Peer Streaming Peer Protocol · Train communication · Streaming multimedia · Peer-to-peer communication

1 Introduction

The amount of data transferred by mobile devices is growing at a high rate. According to the Ericsson Mobility Report [1], data usage by smartphone users is growing at 40% compounded annual growth rate (CAGR). The CAGR of video streaming data to mobile devices is 62% and that of audio streaming is 45% according to the Virtual Networking Index report [2] by Cisco. Between 30 and 40% of users stream video and audio data during their commute [1].

At present, urban rail passengers receive mobile data from cellular networks (see panel A of Fig. 1). During high popularity events (e.g. sports matches, live shows, etc.) cellular network can get overwhelmed by user requests to deliver multimedia data. Urban rail environments serve as a promising candidate for deployment of multimedia distribution systems that can be used to offload cellular networks. As urban rail contains a large number of mostly stationary users in close proximity, it allows for usage of wireless peer-to-peer communication technologies for multimedia data distribution.

© Springer International Publishing AG 2017
A. Pirovano et al. (Eds.): Nets4Cars/Nets4Trains/Nets4Aircraft 2017, LNCS 10222, pp. 41–53, 2017.
DOI: 10.1007/978-3-319-56880-5_5

Furthermore, the availability of radio communication technologies in modern urban rail environments allows for the delivery of bandwidth-intensive data to the train, where it is subsequently distributed to the passengers.

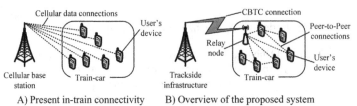

A) Present in-train connectivity   B) Overview of the proposed system

Fig. 1. Present and proposed methods of streaming multimedia distribution to the train passengers

Conventional railway signaling systems, based on color light signals, are rapidly being replaced by modern, electronic systems, widely known as communication-based signaling systems [3, 4]. One of the most notable of such systems is Communications-Based Train Control (CBTC) [5]. In communication-based signaling, a radio communication technology is used to transfer trains control information between a train and the train control center. Nearly all of the modern CBTC systems use IEEE 802.11, widely known as Wi-Fi [6], as the radio technology, mainly owing to its cost-effectiveness [7]. IEEE 802.11a or 802.11g are the most commonly used versions of this technology, supporting data rates of up to 54 Mbps. More advanced versions such as 802.11n and 802.11ac can support even higher rates, up to 1 Gbps.

Using radio communication, CBTC systems enable transfer of real-time and high-resolution train control information between a train and the train control center. CBTC data, which consists of train control messages typically sent about every 500 ms, itself does not require high bandwidth. Typical data rate ranges up to maximum 100 kbps [7]. This leaves with plenty of excessive bandwidth to be used for other purposes.

This work proposes an in-train data distribution system that can be used to distribute streaming multimedia to the train passengers using the unused CBTC radio link bandwidth (see panel B of Fig. 1). Once the multimedia stream is delivered to the train over the CBTC radio connection, it is distributed to the train passenger devices by using peer-to-peer technologies (see Sect. 3 for a detailed description): data connections between the passenger devices are implemented using Wi-Fi Direct [8] and the multimedia data exchange is coordinated by using the Peer-to-Peer Streaming Peer Protocol [9]. While all types of data can be delivered using P2P communication paradigm, this work focuses on streaming multimedia, as it is the biggest driver of mobile data usage.

The goal of this work is to evaluate the proposed in-train multimedia delivery solution. The evaluation is performed by emulating the system, to establish the highest number of concurrent users that can receive the same live High-Definition (HD 720p) multimedia stream. Furthermore, during the system tests, three parameters impacting the streaming multimedia user's experience (see Sect. 5 for a detailed description) were observed: the playback index, the amount of video data skipped and the time until the first frame is rendered.

This work considers streaming multimedia delivery to a single train-car. A train-set with multiple cars could have the proposed system installed in each train-car. While this work considers data distribution performance, it leaves data security and integrity issues for future research.

2   Related Research

The prior research related to the proposed multimedia distribution is grouped into two groups. The first group lists research related to the connectivity methods and deployment scenarios. The second group contains an overview of the group communication protocols.

Research in the first group considers wireless multicast communication. Multicast is a one-to-many communication paradigm, well suited to implement data distribution to a group of users. The authors of [10] propose to deliver multimedia content to the Wi-Fi users via the system called DirCast. Their system uses infrastructure (Access Point) based Wi-Fi connections and requires that the clients' wireless adapters are set to the promiscuous mode. The authors tested the DirCast system with up to 12 users and concluded that DirCast is well suited for streaming media delivery. The authors of [11] investigate the applicability of the IEEE 802.11b/g/n technologies for multicast-based multimedia streaming. The evaluations are based on the mean opinion score of the evaluators. Test results showed that connections using 802.11 g and 802.11n technologies can be used for multicast-based multimedia delivery. However, the achieved data rate differed between Wi-Fi adapters from different manufacturers, even if the adapters supported the same Wi-Fi standard. The authors of [12] consider Wi-Fi based multicast deployment in high-speed trains. In contrast to the work presented here, they consider WiMAX technology to deliver the media stream to the train. The early results indicate that while their approach is feasible, it suffers from a high packet loss.

Research considering Wi-Fi Direct as a communication technology is limited, compared to research considering Wi-Fi based multicast. Authors of [13] presented an in-depth Wi-Fi Direct technology overview and conducted experiments using Wi-Fi Direct to offload 3G (HSDPA) based connections between two computers. Their results show that Wi-Fi Direct is a viable solution for short-range device-to-device communication, achieving data rates up to 3 times higher than using a 3G cellular connection. Research presented in [14] use analytical and simulation analysis to show that Wi-Fi Direct can be used to offload LTE-based cellular connections between the devices in close proximity.

The second group of related work considers application layer multicast (ALM) protocols that can be used to implement one-to-many group communication. Authors of [15] survey ALM protocols specifically designed for live peer-to-peer video streaming. The multimedia distribution system presented in this work uses one of the surveyed protocols: Peer-to-Peer Streaming Peer Protocol [9] (PPSPP). PPSPP is based on the Swift protocol. The authors of [16] provide an in-depth analysis of the Swift protocol features, while the authors of [17] provide a performance analysis of the Swift protocol. The PPSPP protocol specification allows the protocol implementer to choose any data transmission scheduling algorithm. Authors of [18] provide examples of several of such algorithms along with their performance evaluation.

3   Architecture Overview

The proposed in-train multimedia distribution system is implemented using two core technologies to deliver multimedia data to the train passengers. Data connections between the passengers are implemented using the Wi-Fi Direct technology and the multimedia sharing is coordinated using the Peer-to-Peer Streaming Peer Protocol. This section describes the details of both technologies and then presents the overall architecture of the in-train multimedia distribution system.

3.1   Wi-Fi Direct

In the conventional, infrastructure mode of IEEE 802.11 Wi-Fi, two devices placed side by side must connect to an Access Point (AP) in order to be able to communicate to each other, as shown in panel A of Fig. 2. The AP, in this case, is often a dedicated hardware with a superior set of capabilities. An AP is responsible for implementing functionalities such as security, power saving and QoS in the Basic Service Set (BSS), and connects the BSS to the infrastructure network.

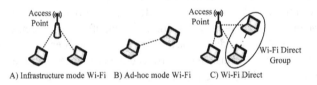

A) Infrastructure mode Wi-Fi   B) Ad-hoc mode Wi-Fi   C) Wi-Fi Direct

Fig. 2. Different modes of Wi-Fi deployment

Users like to share content and services on their personal devices as they interact with other users on the go, without the need for first connecting to an AP [19]. Hence the need for device-to-device (D2D) communication in today's highly dynamic world is rapidly growing. While the 802.11 Wi-Fi has been around for almost two decades now, the D2D communication it supports with its infrastructure-less mode (also known as "ad-hoc mode", shown in panel B of Fig. 2) is far from trivial to use [19]. Furthermore, since infrastructure-less mode does not involve an AP, it lacks the above-mentioned functionalities normally implemented by an AP.

In Wi-Fi Direct, communication takes places in the form of groups. In a P2P Group, a Wi-Fi Direct device—referred to as a P2P Device—can have the role of a P2P Group Owner (GO) or a P2P Client. These roles are negotiated when the group is formed. A GO—also referred to as a "Soft AP" occasionally—provides AP-like functionalities to its clients, both legacy (i.e. conventional 802.11 devices) and P2P clients [19]. GO is as well responsible for running a DHCP server to assign IP addresses to the clients. Like in a conventional Wi-Fi network, a P2P Group has an SSID. This SSID always starts with ASCII characters "Direct-" to distinguish itself from conventional Wi-Fi SSIDs [8].

One may argue that Wi-Fi Direct is not a peer-to-peer technology in its true sense as there exist hierarchical roles (GO and clients). This is a contrast to the conventional ad-hoc networking where all devices are equal, without any hierarchies.

A Wi-Fi device must support IEEE 802.11 g or a newer technology to be able to act as P2P Device [8]. A P2P Device can assume both roles (GO and Client) if it has multiple wireless interfaces, or if it can implement virtual interfaces or time-sharing techniques on the same interface [19]. Likewise, a P2P Device can be both a part of a Wi-Fi Direct group and maintain a conventional Wi-Fi connection simultaneously, as shown in panel C of Fig. 2. Such a device is referred to as a P2P Concurrent Device [8, 13, 19]. This enables a wide range of possibilities. For example, a P2P Device can provide a connection to the outer world by simultaneously connecting to a conventional Wi-Fi AP or a 3G/4G network and to a P2P Client. This is a major advantage over conventional ad-hoc networking in which devices cannot simultaneously connect to existing Wi-Fi networks. Additionally, a P2P Device can be a member of multiple P2P Groups simultaneously [8].

Thus, in contrast to a conventional Wi-Fi network in which a device can either operate as an AP or a client, in Wi-Fi Direct, these roles are arbitrary—any device can function as an AP. Furthermore, the fact that this new capability can be implemented entirely in software, without a need of making any changes to the existing 802.11 hardware, bears a high significance [13].

3.2 Peer-to-Peer Streaming Peer Protocol

Streaming multimedia distribution to and between the train passengers is coordinated by using the Peer-to-Peer Streaming Peer Protocol [9] (PPSPP). PPSPP is an Internet Engineering Task Force standardized protocol used to implement peer-to-peer based data distribution.

Each train passenger using the in-train streaming multimedia distribution system has to run a client of PPSPP protocol software. The client software can be run on any computing device, like a laptop, a smartphone or a tablet. A group of connected users that are running the PPSPP clients is referred to as a swarm. After starting the PPSPP client, each member of a swarm makes a TCP connection to the tracker node. The tracker node is used by the arriving nodes to learn IP addresses of other members in the swarm and to get the bootstrap information required to start downloading data. The tracker node functionality can be implemented in a dedicated node or in one of the swarm members.

PPSPP works by dividing the shared data into fixed size pieces called chunks. Each client participating in the peer-to-peer data exchange periodically informs other clients about data chunks it has. It does so by sending one or more "HAVE" messages to all other connected clients. Each "HAVE" message contains a continuous range of chunks numbers that the client shares. Upon reception of the "HAVE" message, each client compares the range of chunks advertised in the "HAVE" message to the list of chunks available locally by the receiving client. If the sending client has chunks that are not available at the receiving client, the receiving client sends a "REQUEST" message to the sender of the "HAVE" messages, requesting the range of chunks not available at the receiving client. Upon receiving a "REQUEST" message, a client starts sending the requested data chunks to the sender of the "REQUEST" message.

In the proposed system, multimedia data is 'injected' into the PPSPP swarm by a special node called the root node. Functionally, the root node is identical to the other nodes in the swarm running an instance of the PPSPP protocol. The only difference is that in the proposed system, tracker functionality was implemented in the same node as root node.

Clients in a swarm can use either TCP or UDP to communicate and exchange data chunks. When PPSPP is used with TCP protocol, repeating failed chunk transmissions is handled by the TCP protocol. Using UDP with PPSPP requires the implementer to design a custom automatic repeat request (ARQ) algorithm to reschedule failed chunk transmissions. To streamline the operation of the PPSPP clients, the in-train multimedia distribution system uses TCP protocol. When PPSPP is used to distribute streaming multimedia, each client can be configured with a discard window, indicating the number of data chunks that each client will hold and make available to other nodes before discarding them. Using a discard window reduces the memory requirements in the PPSPP clients, as each client keeps no more chunks than the size of the discard window.

3.3 Multimedia Distribution System Architecture

The overall multimedia distribution system architecture consists of a single radio connection to the train-car, the root node, and the in-train Wi-Fi Direct network, as shown in Fig. 3.

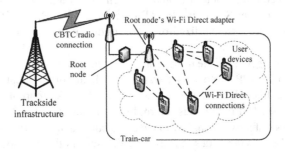

Fig. 3. Architecture of the proposed in-train multimedia streaming system

The multimedia stream is delivered to the train-car by utilizing the unused bandwidth of the CBTC radio connection. Nevertheless, the exact technology of the connection (Wi-Fi, LTE, IEEE802.11p, etc.) does not impact the functioning of the multimedia delivery system, as long as the connection can maintain the required data rate.

Once the multimedia stream is delivered to the train-car, it is received by the root node. The root node acts as a proxy server, receiving the multimedia stream and sharing it using the PPSPP protocol. The root node can be implemented using a commodity computer hardware. The requirements for the root node hardware are that it must support the same radio technology as used by the CBTC connection, must be able to interface with the Wi-Fi network card supporting the Wi-Fi Direct protocol, and must be able to run an instance of the client software implementing the PPSPP protocol.

The train passengers can join the Wi-Fi Direct network by using a device supporting the Wi-Fi Direct connectivity (supported in systems running Android 4.0+ and MS Windows 8+) and having a client application installed on their devices. The application can be configured to join the local Wi-Fi Direct network by scanning a QR code located in the train-car or by using other location-based configuration methods. In addition to configuring the device's Wi-Fi Direct connectivity, the application acts as a client of the PPSPP protocol.

Once the train passenger's device is configured to join the Wi-Fi Direct network, it registers with the tracker node and starts making connections to other users. As soon as the first Wi-Fi Direct connection is established (either to the root node or to another user), the passenger starts receiving video data which is rendered on the device's screen. The proposed system has a single tracker node, co-located with the root node. For simplicity, other nodes in the system (passenger devices) never perform tracker node's functions.

4   Experimental Setup

To evaluate the proposed in-train streaming multimedia distribution system, a series of system emulations were performed. This section describes the experimental setup.

The multimedia distribution system was evaluated by using the CORE network emulator [20] with Extendable Mobile Ad-hoc Network Emulator (EMANE) [21]. The CORE network emulator uses Linux Containers (LXC) to divide the host computer running the CORE software into a number of independent virtual hosts, each running the Linux operating system. In our experiments, a virtual host represented a single train passenger using the multimedia distribution system. Each virtual train passenger ran an instance of the PPSPP protocol client[1]. Network emulation software ran in a server-grade workstation to reduce any negative impact of the availability of computational resources on emulation results. Each emulation scenario was repeated 3 times and the results were averaged.

The EMANE emulator was used to emulate the media access (MAC) and physical (PHY) layers of the Wi-Fi Direct protocol. The MAC layer used the IEEE 802.11g standard with the maximum data rate set to 54 Mbps. The Wi-Fi Direct connections were modeled by using the infrastructure-less Wi-Fi mode. In the current setup, all nodes use the same Wi-Fi channel to transmit data. In future work, multiple non-overlapping Wi-Fi radio channels will be used for communication between the nodes. This approach should minimize radio interference among the users and allow for a larger number of concurrent users.

Testing of the system used a model data source having the same data production rate as the VP8 video codec [22]. VP8 is a royalty-free video codec developed by Google and released to the public domain. The data rate of the codec was 2 Mbps and the video

---

[1] Source code available at http://github.com/justas-/PyPPSPP.

size of 1280 × 720 pixels (also known as HD 720p). The frame rate was set to 10 frames per second. The average key frame size was 29 301 B, and the average size of a non-key frame was 6 030 B. Audio data was encoded using "Vorbis" codec with an average frame size of 1 601 B.

5   Results Analysis and Evaluation

The proposed multimedia distribution solution was evaluated in a series of deployment scenarios using the CORE network emulator software. Each scenario varied by the number of users (between 14 and 20) and the number of concurrent connections each user maintained to other users (between 4 and 10). The following section describes the analyzed parameters and presents the experimental results. The analyzed parameters impacting user's experience were the playback index, the amount of skipped data and the time until the first frame is rendered.

5.1   Playback Index

In video streaming systems, video data is delivered to the clients divided into frames. The frames are then rendered on the device's screen by the video decoder at a constant frame rate. The playback index is the ratio of the number of frames rendered successfully to the number of render attempts. If the video decoder always has enough data in the buffer to render the next frame, the number of successful attempts is equal to the render attempts and the playback index is 1 (or 100%). From the streaming video user's perspective, a playback index of 100% corresponds to a video stream that is rendered without interruptions. The observed playback index in different emulated scenarios is shown in Fig. 4.

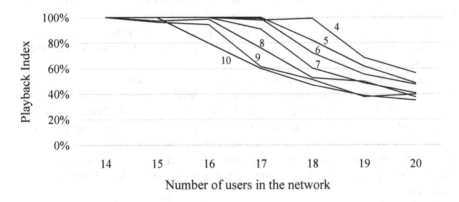

Fig. 4. Average playback index observed in test scenarios. Each line indicates the number of concurrent connections between users

The playback index is directly related to the availability of video data that is to be rendered. As Fig. 4 shows, the playback index (and the availability of video data) is linked to the number of users in the network and the number of concurrent connections each user maintains to other users. As shown in the figure, the proposed system can support up to 15 concurrent users, while maintaining the playback index at 100%. The number of concurrent users can be increased to 18 without affecting the playback index by reducing the number of parallel connection each user maintains from 10 to 4.

The number of concurrent users is practically limited due to the users contending for the shared transmission medium. Each user actively transmitting data over the Wi-Fi Direct connection acts as a source of interference to the other users. Increasing the number of concurrent users increases the total amount of interference, which in turn reduces the rate of successful data transmissions between the users. This, in turn, reduces the availability of video data to the video decoder and reduces the playback index.

The number of concurrent connections a user maintains to other users has a similar effect on the playback index as the number of users in the network. Each concurrent connection is used to periodically exchange chunks availability information between the users. As the number of concurrent connections increases, each user transmits data more often, thus interfering with transmissions of the other users.

The number of concurrent users in the network can be increased (without reducing the playback index) by limiting the interference each user creates to other users. As mentioned above, in future, the user model will be upgraded to establish connections using multiple non-overlapping Wi-Fi channels to limit interference.

5.2 Skipped Data

All users in the proposed multimedia delivery system maintained a discard window of 1000 chunks. As described in Sect. 3.2, maintaining a discard window reduces the user's memory requirements. Since all users maintain the discard window individually, it is possible for the user's video decoder to get stuck by waiting for the frame that is already discarded by all remaining users in the swarm. In such case, user's video decoder has been programmed in a way that after 10th unsuccessful attempts to render a frame (video freeze of 1 s), it skips the following 250 chunks (the size of playback buffer) and continues rendering the video data. From the viewer's perspective, skipped data is seen as a jump forward in the playback of the video. The average chunk production rate of the video source was 80 chunks per second, hence each jump of 250 chunks corresponded to skipping of approximately 3,125 s of video data. The average number of skipped data chunks in the experiments is shown in Fig. 5.

The skipping of data chunks is caused by the video decoder being unable to decode the next frame in 10 consecutive attempts, due to the unavailability of video data. As such, the observed results follow closely the results of the playback index discussed in the previous section. The key cause of data being unavailable is users' contention for shared transmission medium and subsequent unsuccessful data transmissions.

As seen in Fig. 5, the proposed multimedia distribution system can deliver video data without skipping any data chunks to 14 users. The number of concurrent users that received video data and does not skip any data chunks can be further increased to 18 by reducing the number of connections that each user maintains to other users.

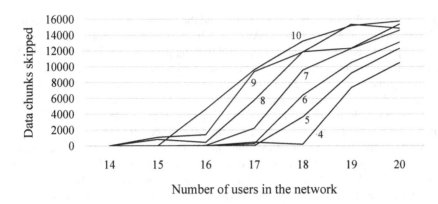

Fig. 5. Average number of skipped data chunks. Each line indicates the number of concurrent connections between users

The number of discarded data chunks can be decreased by reducing the interference in Wi-Fi Direct data transmissions between the users (as explained in the previous section) and by employing more advanced chunk skipping algorithms. In the current chunk skipping algorithm, users skip 250 chunks after a 10th consecutive unsuccessful attempt to render a video frame. A future version of the chunks skipping algorithm would skip missing chunks until a continuous block of data chunks of a certain size is found. Likewise, at the moment, if the unavailable chunks are delivered after they have been skipped, they are discarded. In future, a feature of cancelling the request for the chunks that have already been skipped will be considered.

5.3   Time to the First Frame

The last analyzed parameter is the length of the time period between the time a user's device starts joining the multimedia distribution system and the time the device renders the first frame. During this time period, the PPSPP client on the user's device is initialized, registers with the tracker node, learns about available data, connects to other devices (either other users or the root node), and receives enough data to fill the initial playback buffer (250 data chunks). The observed time to the first frame is shown in Fig. 6. For brevity, only the results for 4 to 8 concurrent connections are shown.

As seen in Fig. 6, the time period until the first frame is rendered increases with the size of the network. The average time to the first frame in the network of 14 users is 12.5 s, while in the network of 20 users it increases to 17.9 s. The average time to the first frame varies only slightly in the scenarios where each user maintains 6 or more concurrent connections to other users. On the other hand, it varies greatly in the scenarios where each user maintains only 4 or 5 concurrent connections to other users.

Overall the time to the first frame is generally long (between 12 and 17 s). The main cause of the long delay in the scenarios with 4 or 5 concurrent connections is the time required to find a node that can accept a connection. When each node is configured to maintain only a small number of connections, the probability of finding a node that can accept a new connection is lower.

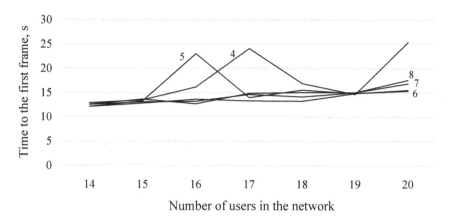

Fig. 6. Time to the first frame. Each line indicates the number of concurrent connections between users.

The time to the first frame can be reduced by finding a user that can accept a new connection faster. In the current version of the proposed system, each new user receives a list of other users in the swarm when it registers with the tracker-node. In a future version, each node might periodically report to the tracker node the number of free connection slots it has. The tracker then could include this information with a list of current users in the swarm that is sent to all new users.

6   Conclusions

This work evaluated a multimedia distribution system for use in urban rail environments. The proposed system uses Communications-Based Train Control radio link's unused bandwidth to deliver the multimedia stream to the train-car, where it is subsequently distributed to the train passengers using the peer-to-peer technologies.

The proposed system was tested using computer network emulation techniques. The results indicate that up to 14 users can concurrently receive the same high-definition (HD 720p) multimedia stream. The number of concurrent users can be increased to 18 by reducing the number of connections that each user maintains to other users from 10 to 4. The results with more than 18 concurrent users indicate that the user's experience, as measured by the playback index and the amount of discarded video data, falls sharply as the number of concurrent users increases further.

The evaluation results show that the proposed system can be used only in situations where the number of train passengers in a single train-car is limited. The main cause being that each user acts as a source of interference to other users during data transmissions. Future work is needed to improve the maximum number of users supported by the proposed system. Nevertheless, it shall be noted that the total number of train passengers that can use the system can be increased by deploying multiple instances of the system, e.g. one in each train-car.

In future work, the proposed system will use multiple non-overlapping Wi-Fi channels to deliver data between the users, reducing the radio interference between the users. Furthermore, advanced versions of data skipping and connections establishment algorithms will be researched to further improve the user experience of the system.

References

1. Ericsson Mobility Report - Western Europe. Ericsson (2016)
2. Cisco VNI Mobile Forecast (2015 – 2020). Cisco (2016)
3. Strategic Analysis of Communications-Based Train Control Systems in the Western European Urban Rail Market. Frost & Sullivan (2013)
4. Sector Overview and Competitiveness Survey of the Railway Supply Industry. European Commission (2012)
5. IEEE Standard for Communications-Based Train Control (CBTC) Performance and Functional Requirements (2004)
6. IEEE Standard for Information technology - Telecommunications and information exchange between systems Local and metropolitan area networks. Part 11: Wireless LAN Medium Access Control (MAC) and Physical Layer (PHY) Specifications (2016)
7. Farooq, J., Soler, J.: Radio communication for communications-based train control (CBTC): a tutorial and survey. IEEE Commun. Surv. Tutorials 1 (2017)
8. Wi-Fi Peer-to-Peer (P2P) Technical Specification Version 1.7. Wi-Fi Alliance (2016)
9. Bakker, A., Petrocco, R., Grishchenko, V.: Peer-to-peer streaming peer protocol (PPSPP). IETF RFC7574 (2015)
10. Chandra, R., Karanth, S., Moscibroda, T., Navda, V., Padhye, J., Ramjee, R., Ravindranath, L.: DirCast: a practical and efficient Wi-Fi multicast system. In: 2009 17th IEEE International Conference on Network Protocols, pp. 161–170. IEEE (2009)
11. Kostuch, A., Gierłowski, K., Wozniak, J.: Performance analysis of multicast video streaming in IEEE 802.11 b/g/n testbed environment. In: Wozniak, J., Konorski, J., Katulski, R., Pach, Andrzej R. (eds.) WMNC 2009. IAICT, vol. 308, pp. 92–105. Springer, Heidelberg (2009). doi:10.1007/978-3-642-03841-9_9
12. Chiao, H., Chang, S., Li, K., Kuo, Y., Tseng, M.: WiFi multicast streaming using AL-FEC inside the trains of high-speed rails (2010)
13. Camps-Mur, D., Garcia-Saavedra, A., Serrano, P.: Device-to-device communications with Wi-Fi Direct: overview and experimentation. IEEE Wirel. Commun. 20, 96–104 (2013)
14. Pyattaev, A., Galinina, O., Johnsson, K., Surak, A., Florea, R., Andreev, S., Koucheryavy, Y.: Network-assisted D2D over WiFi direct. In: Mumtaz, S., Rodriguez, J. (eds.) Smart Device to Smart Device Communication, pp. 165–218. Springer, Cham (2014). doi: 10.1007/978-3-319-04963-2_7
15. Zhang, X., Hassanein, H.: A survey of peer-to-peer live video streaming schemes - an algorithmic perspective. Comput. Netw. 56, 3548–3579 (2012)
16. Osmani, F., Grishchenko, V., Jimenez, R., Knutsson, B.: Swift: the missing link between peer-to-peer and information-centric networks. In: Proceedings of Work. P2P Dependability, pp. 1–6 (2012)
17. Petrocco, R., Pouwelse, J., Epema, D.H.J.: Performance analysis of the Libswift P2P streaming protocol. In: 2012 IEEE 12th International Conference Peer-to-Peer Computing P2P 2012, Pp. 103–114 (2012)
18. Vlavianos, A., Iliofotou, M., Faloutsos, M.: BiToS: enhancing BitTorrent for supporting streaming applications. In: Proceedings - IEEE INFOCOM (2006)

19. Conti, M., Delmastro, F., Minutiello, G., Paris, R.: Experimenting opportunistic networks with WiFi Direct. In: Proceedings of IFIP Wireless Days (2013)
20. Ahrenholz, J.: Comparison of CORE network emulation platforms. In: Proceedings - IEEE Military Communications Conference MILCOM, pp. 166–171 (2010)
21. Extendable Mobile Ad-hoc Network Emulator (EMANE). https://www.nrl.navy.mil/itd/ncs/products/emane
22. Bankoski, J., Wilkins, P., Xu, Y.: Technical overview of VP8, an open source video codec for the web. In: Proceedings - IEEE International Conference Multimedia Expo (2011)

High-Speed Railway Composite Scenarios: Power Delay Profiles and Time-Dispersion Analysis

Lei Zhang[1], Juan Moreno[1(✉)], César Briso[1], and Ke Guan[2]

[1] ETSIS Telecomunicación, Universidad Politécnica de Madrid, UPM, Madrid, Spain
juanmorenogl@diac.upm.es
[2] State Key Lab of Railway Traffic and Control, Beijing Jiaotong University, Beijing, China

Abstract. This paper presents a series of wideband channel sounder measurements carried out in a High-Speed Railway (HSR) composite scenario. The composite scenario involves a tunnel, a cutting and a viaduct, which are three of the most common special scenarios in this type of lines. The Power Delay Profile (PDP) is also analyzed to generate the Tapped-Delay Lines (TDL) channel models in different regions.

Keywords: High-Speed railway · Measurements · Propagation · Wireless

1 Introduction

In high-speed railways (HSR) the throughput of the wireless systems is limited by speed of the vehicle. The current world speed record for HSR is 574.8 km/h and was achieved by an Alstom train on a SNCF track in 2007. As we move forward to 5G, the research on wireless faces new challenges. The most critical one is how to provide a high capacity wireless system on a HSR scenario, to support railway services like ERTMS, real-time CCTV, infotainment, Internet access for passengers and a large etcetera [1].

One of the most important features of HSR scenarios is the fast fading caused by the large relative speed (this is, Doppler spread) [2]. Moreover, Doppler spreads are time-varying so it means also a non-stationary fading channel. The Doppler shift causes a misalignment of the frequencies of transmitter and receiver. This misalignment can decrease the subcarrier orthogonality and cause Inter-Carrier Interference in OFDM systems. Moreover, as the speed of the train increases, the assumption of having a perfect knowledge of the channel (as in low mobility scenarios) is no longer valid [2]. This means that the performance of the whole wireless system could decrease significantly. For all these reasons, channel modeling techniques are very important in an HSR environment.

Several measurement campaigns have been taken in different HSR scenarios, like viaducts [3], hilly terrains [4] cuttings [5], train stations [6] and tunnels [7]. The empirical results analysis and statistical modeling in large-scale and small-scale have been conducted based on these measurements.

The structure of this article is as follows: Sect. 2 provides an overview of the HSR environment where the measurements were taken; Sect. 3 presents the results and in Sect. 4 the conclusions are drawn.

A. Pirovano et al. (Eds.): Nets4Cars/Nets4Trains/Nets4Aircraft 2017, LNCS 10222, pp. 54–59, 2017.
DOI: 10.1007/978-3-319-56880-5_6

2   Environment

Most of the research work aforementioned is dedicated to explain a unique scenario (cutting, or viaduct, or tunnel, etc.). In fact, real railway lines are formed by the combination of all these unique scenarios. This is of special importance when the train moves at a high speed, because the transition from one scenario to other is done very quickly. So, these regions with different topographies cannot be separated easily. We say that a scenario formed by many unique scenarios is a composite scenario. The existing research has not considered the transitions between two scenarios. Therefore, the non-stationary of fast varying channels in these HSR composite scenarios requires further research.

To measure the wireless channel a portable channel sounder is used. It operates generating a train of periodic narrow pulses. The distorted signal is received by the channel sounder receiver. After the envelope detection, the demodulated signal is sent to the digital oscilloscope (Keysight Infiniium MSO9104A). Further details about the channel sounder can be found in Table 1.

Table 1. Channel sounder parameters

Parameter	Description
Frequency	950 MHz/2150 MHz
Transmitting power	35 dBm
Pulse width/period	30 ns/1 us
IF bandwidth	100 MHz
Noise figure	3 dB
Sensitivity	−100 dBm
Sample interval	50 ns

Moreover, the channel sounder transmitter is equipped with a directional antenna (L-Com HG727 14P-090); whereas on the receiver side we have an omnidirectional antenna (L-Com HG72107U). Both of them are vertical polarized (see Table 2 for further details about the antennas).

Table 2. Antenna parameters

Item	Transmitter antenna	Receiver antenna
Frequency range	698–960/1710–2700 MHz	
Gain	13/14 dBi	4/7 dBi
Vertical beamwidth	17°	55°
Horizontal beamwidth	90°	360°
Polarization	Vertical	
Front to back ratio	> 23 dB	–
Height	3 m	1 m
Dimensions	1568 * 320 * 160 mm	Length: 1.02 m

The composite scenario where the measurements were taken has a viaduct and a deep cutting. In Fig. 1 a sketch of the composite scenario is depicted. The cuttings shape can imply a significant number of reflections and some scattering as well. Viaducts (usually with a height of 10–30 m) are also used in HSR to avoid slopes in the track which undermine train's high speed. It is very common to raise the antennas in the viaduct to maintain the LOS between transmitter and receiver, as well as decreasing the number of scatters that can affect the signal. Therefore, cutting and viaduct have opposite effects on the channel. All these effects imply the impossibility to model the propagation in a HSR environment as a pure LOS channel.

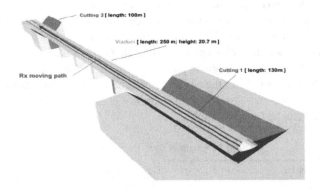

Fig. 1. Composite scenario. Tunnel entrance, cutting, viaduct and another cutting.

The wideband measurements have been conducted in a composite scenario, which is located in the "Datong-Xi'an" HSR line (Xinzhou, Shanxi Province, China). The composite scenario starts at the end of a tunnel and is formed by a 130-m long cutting (immediately after the tunnel), followed by a viaduct of 250 m and, finally another cutting of 100 m (Fig. 1, from right to the left). So we have four regions in our scenario: region 1, near to the tunnel, where the cutting causes a lot of multipath; region 2, the first cutting where the two steep walls can reflect the transmitting waves and create some multipath; region 3, the viaduct, with almost no multipath (is an open area); and finally, region IV where the second cutting is located.

This composite scenario is very representative of the typical HSR environments where the main scatters are located near the track. The receiver is located on the track 30 m away from the transmitter (see Fig. 2). To take the measurements the receiver is moved along the track taking average power-delay-profiles at 50 different positions (distance between transmitter and receiver varies from 30 m to 458 m). To evaluate the effects of multipath on the channel in a composite scenario like this one we have taken a set of wideband measurements at 950 MHz and 2150 MHz.

3   Results

We provide two different results: power-delay profiles and time dispersion analysis at the two frequencies considered (950 and 2150 MHz). Power-delay profiles are very useful to characterize the fading.

Fig. 2. Measurement setup. The receiver is over the track and the transmitter is 30 m away (on the right)

3.1 Power-Delay Profile

In the area close to the tunnel a NLOS scenario is presented in region 1. PDPs at both frequencies display a weak main component and a large delay (see Fig. 3a). In particular, the delay spread at 950 MHz is larger and more multipath happens at 950 MHz than at 2150 MHz. In region 2 we are in a stronger LOS scenario with little delay spread (see Fig. 3b). In region 3 the LOS component is attenuated, but the impact of cutting 1 is still present. Therefore, the PDP in Fig. 3c has similar multipath components with also weak dominant LOS components. In Fig. 3d, which corresponds also to region 3 (viaduct) multipath components are very weak due to the lack of surface to reflect the signal, and consequently, the delay spread is much lower. Once we move to the other side of the viaduct towards cutting 2, the LOS components decrease as the separation between transmitter and receiver increases. Equally, we start receiving reflections from cutting 2, which implies more delay spread (see Fig. 3e). In cutting 2 there is only one path (see Fig. 3f). This is because the size of this cutting is smaller than cutting 1 and has an asymmetry with lower height, so the time delay caused by the multipath components is very short and close to the LOS component.

3.2 Time-Dispersion Analysis

To analyze the delay spread on a wideband measurement, a valid method is to estimate the excess delay and RMS delay spread. These two parameters characterize the time dispersive nature of the channel and can as well be used to determine the number of channel taps. The excess delay is the maximum delay above a threshold which reveals the maximum relative distance between the receiver and the reflection or scattering surfaces. The RMS delay spread is the square root of the second central moment of the power-delay profile.

The average excess delay, average RMS delay spread and average number of channel taps in each region are summarized in Table 3. The RMS delay along the measurement points at 950 MHz and 2150 MHz is presented in Fig. 4.

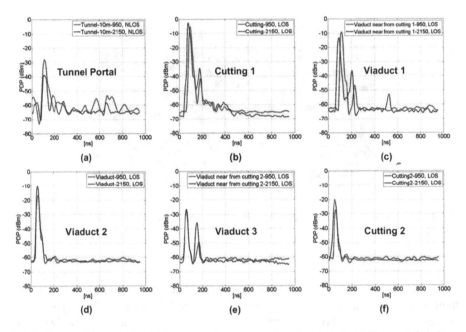

Fig. 3. Power-delay profiles in (a) tunnel entrance; (b) cutting 1; (c) viaduct 1 (the part of viaduct close to cutting 1); (d) middle of the viaduct (viaduct 2); (e) the part of viaduct close to cutting 2 (Viaduct 3); (f) cutting 2.

Table 3. Time dispersion results

Region		1	2	3	4
Avg. excess delay (ns)	950 MHz	270.1	105.6	36.8	21.7
	2150 MHz	165.3	129.6	31.2	31.3
Avg. RMS delay spread (ns)	950 MHz	106.4	32.6	5.3	16.2
	2150 MHz	71.3	43.3	7.5	13.7
Number of channel taps	950 MHz	4–5	2	1	1–2
	2150 MHz	3–4	2	1	1–2

The variation of the RMS delay spread through the track is interpreted as an evidence of the aforementioned results. The multipath components on each region of the composite scenario are different. In particular as we move from the entrance of the tunnel and cutting 1 (region 1) to an open area (viaduct), the average RMS delay decreases 1 magnitude order (from 70–100 ns to 5–7 ns). Also the number of channel taps decreases significantly. However, average excess delay in region 4 (cutting 2) is smaller than in region 3, but the RMS delay values are just the opposite.

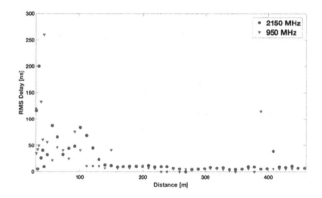

Fig. 4. RMS delay spread at 900 MHz and 2150 MHz

4 Conclusion

We present some measurements on a composite scenario of a high-speed railway line. This composite scenario is very representative as this type of lines are not straight and flat countryside tracks, but more complex layouts with viaducts, tunnels, cuttings and other geographical features. The most relevant parameters to analyze the time dispersion properties have been extracted. These parameters are the excess delay, the RMS delay spread, and the number of channel taps. Furthermore, the TDL channel models can be established in detail in different regions.

Acknowledgment. The authors want to express their acknowledgements to the project ENABLING 5G reference TEC2014-55735-C3-2-R of the Spanish Research Agency, Minister of Economy and Competitiveness.

References

1. Moreno, J., Manuel Riera, J., de Haro, L., Rodríguez, C.: A survey on the future railway radio communications services: challenges and opportunities. IEEE Commun. Mag. **53**, 62–68 (2015)
2. Ai, B., Cheng, X., Kürner, T., Zhong, Z.-D., Guan, K., He, R.-S., Xiong, L., Matolak, D.W., Michelson, D.G., Briso-Rodriguez, C.: Challenges toward wireless communications for high-speed railway. IEEE Trans. Intell. Transp. Syst. **15**(5), 2143–2158 (2014)
3. He, R., Zhong, Z., Ai, B., Ding, J.: An empirical path loss model and fading analysis for high-speed railway viaduct scenarios. IEEE Antennas Wirel. Propag. Lett. **10**(10), 808–812 (2011)
4. Luan, F., Zhang, Y., Xiao, L., Zhou, C., Zhou, S.: Fading characteristics of wireless channel on high-speed railway in hilly terrain scenario. Int. J. Antennas Propag. (2013)
5. He, R., Zhong, Z., Ai, B., Ding, J., Yang, Y., Molisch., A.F.: Short-term fading behavior in high-speed railway cutting scenario: measurements, analysis, and statistical models. IEEE Trans. Antennas Propag. **61**(4), 2209–2222 (2013)
6. Guan, K., Zhong, Z., Ai, B.: Empirical models for extra propagation loss of train stations on high-speed railway. IEEE Trans. Antennas Propag. **62**(3), 1395–1408 (2014)
7. Briso-Rodrguez, C., Cruz, J.M., Alonso, J.I.: Measurements and modeling of distributed antenna systems in railway tunnels. IEEE Trans. Veh. Technol. **56**(5), 2870–2879 (2007)

Throughput Performance of 3GPP LTE System in Railway Environment

Loïc Brunel$^{(\boxtimes)}$, Hervé Bonneville, and Akl Charaf

Mitsubishi Electric R&D Centre Europe, Rennes, France
`l.brunel@fr.merce.mee.com`

Abstract. The design of the next train radio telecommunication system has started in Europe, based on initiatives at International Railway Union (UIC), European Railway Agency (ERA) and European Telecommunications Standards Institute (ETSI). This new system must satisfy rail community requirements and replace the currently used GSM-R (Global System for Mobile communications - Railways) system. The 3GPP LTE (Third Generation Partnership Project - Long Term Evolution) mobile cellular system and its evolutions are among the candidates and must be evaluated for railway services. This paper aims at providing an overview of current standardization work and system-level evaluation results of LTE in a railway environment.

1 Introduction

Designing a specific radio communication system for railways guarantees that railway-specific requirements are satisfied. However, a specific design has some cost impact. Besides, interoperability is necessary in Europe to allow trains to seamlessly cross state borders. Hence, it is attractive to benefit from designs and developments made for other purposes, like cellular public access. However, the evolution pace of systems in railway field is much slower than in public access. Targets and requirements are different even if 3GPP (Third Generation Partnership), standardizing mobile cellular systems, has the intention to address vertical sectors (e.g., transport, energy, e-health, factory automation) in future releases. In Europe, several initiatives are going on at International Railway Union (UIC), European Railway Agency (ERA) and European Telecommunications Standards Institute (ETSI) to prepare the next train radio telecommunication system that would fit rail community requirements in replacement of current GSM-R (Global System for Mobile communications - Railways) system. Evolutions of 3GPP LTE (Long Term Evolution) are candidates but 5G could also jump in the list [1]. Based on requirements set by UIC, an evaluation work has started at ETSI, first looking at the available LTE standard. After providing an overview of current railway and 3GPP status in Sect. 2, the paper will describe how LTE standard can be deployed to target high speed train applications in Sect. 3. Then, the concept of system-level evaluations and the evaluation results themselves will be presented in Sect. 4 and 5, respectively, and finally some conclusions will be drawn in Sect. 6.

© Springer International Publishing AG 2017
A. Pirovano et al. (Eds.): Nets4Cars/Nets4Trains/Nets4Aircraft 2017, LNCS 10222, pp. 60–71, 2017.
DOI: 10.1007/978-3-319-56880-5_7

2 Next Generation of Train Radio Telecommunication System

2.1 GSM-R

In the 90s, the European Union decided to launch a study on a unified train communication system that would facilitate train movement across state borders, in addition to improve signalling and train control required to reduce intervals between trains on dense lines and support high speed trains. Ten years later, ERTMS (European Rail Traffic Management System) was completed. It defines several components, mainly ETCS (European Train Control System), the train control application, and GSM-R, a radio communication part based on GSM and enhanced to support services required for train operation, e.g., group calls, emergency calls, call pre-emption, location-dependent addressing, functional addressing, and direct mode. GSM-R has been adopted in most of the European countries and worldwide on main lines. However, the deployment is slow due to its heavy cost and the long life cycle of railways equipments. Even if GSM-R fulfils railway needs for train control communications, there are two main drivers for an evolution of the radio system. Firstly, railway operators' requirements evolve toward a larger use of the radio communication system with new applications, e.g., CCTV (Closed-Circuit TeleVision) for look-ahead control and on-board monitoring, train maintenance and configuration, enhanced Public Information System (PIS). Using service-dedicated communication systems is costly in terms of deployment and usage, and having one radio able to support all the services would be beneficial. Such a radio system would need to offer bandwidth capacity out of reach of GSM. A second driver is related to upcoming GSM obsolescence. The decreasing of industry chain supporting GSM products will negatively impact the availability, costs and maintenance capability of 2G systems. GSM-R industry promises support at least until 2030. However, taking into account the time for technology evaluation, standardisation, product development, trials, certification and migration, it is time to think about the next generation.

2.2 Preparing Next Generation Train Radio System

There is a huge difference of product life cycle between the public telecommunication industry and the railway industry. Public telecommunication industry produces a new system generation every ten years whereas the railway industry designs its products with a time horizon which is more about thirty years in mind. However, to keep support and to limit maintenance cost, railways cannot completely ignore what happens in the public telecommunication industry. One solution is to use as much as possible off-the-shelf components for the telecommunication system. As railways require specific features and requirements, either the service could be designed as an "over the top" application over a basic radio system which would be robust enough to support it, or should be - at least partly - embedded in the telecommunication system itself and offered as an integrated service. The first approach enforces the independence between the applications and the telecommunication system, which is not always feasible, and cannot benefit from information of the lower communication layers to optimise performance. The second approach results in a more optimised system, but at the cost of more standardisation effort and less flexibility.

In 2009, UIC started thinking about the next train radio communication system. A first document defining a set of technology-independent user requirements a new radio telecommunication system must support was released in October 2010 [2]. In 2014, the Future Railway Mobile Communication System (FRMCS) project was officially launched, aiming at providing a complete information for decisions on the successor of GSM-R. European Union is also active on the topic through ERA which conducted a survey among all railways stakeholders [3] in order to build a common understanding of requirements and possible solutions toward a future radio communication system. Among others, the study mentions 3GPP LTE as a possible basis, but recommends also a monitoring of 3GPP 5G activity. It also recommends a more active implication of rail sector in 3GPP standardisation in order to ensure that its requirements are taken into consideration. In ETSI (European Telecommunications Standards Institute), RT-NG2R group (Railways Telecommunications - Next Generation Radio for Rail) was created in July 2015 to address the requirements from the rail transportation domain (including urban, suburban, regional and long distance rail), to define the related architecture and radio spectrum needs and to identify and fill in standardisation gaps when necessary.

UIC FRMCS and ETSI RT-NG2R are coordinating their actions to influence 3GPP work. This led to the creation of a railways dedicated Study Item (SI) in 3GPP SA1 in June 2016 called 'Study on Future Railway Mobile Communication System' [4], with the goal to define use cases and requirements specific to railways. The SI should be completed by March 2017 [5] and followed by a Work Item phase, with corresponding technical specifications that could be expected by the end of 2017. In parallel, UIC FRMCS and ETSI RT-NG2R should propose a new Study Item to 3GPP SA6, the group in charge of defining application layer functional elements and interfaces to support critical communications. The study would aim to compare the railways specific requirements as specified by 3GPP SA1 to what is offered today by 3GPP mission-critical features, and propose solutions if needed.

ETSI NG2R has also an action on spectrum request for the next-generation train radio communication system. A technical report has been issued [6] in January 2017 examining the amount of spectrum needed and possible spectrum bands that could be used. 3GPP LTE but also 5G are taken as possible technical options to support the FRMCS - the performances of those systems could offer in a railway environment will impact the amount of spectrum that would be needed. At European level, CEPT ECC (European Conference of Postal and Telecommunications Administrations Electronic Communications Committee) has created a dedicated group to examine spectrum for railways services, and ETSI report will be a technical input to that group.

Preparing the next generation means also preparing the migration phase. The time-line shall include end-to-end trials, end-to-end integration, multi-vendor interoperability testing, deployment, co-existence and interoperability between GSM-R and the new system. Considering a possible end of GSM-R from 2030, the new generation should be available in the early 2020s for a safe migration.

Hence, the 3GPP Long Term Evolution (LTE) mobile cellular system and its evolutions are identified as potential candidates for the next train radio communication system. LTE was designed initially as a replacement to UMTS, with a focus on public data and voice mobile broadband (MBB) services. In a 20 MHz radio channel, it can provide peak data rate of 172.8 Mbit/s for 2×2 antennas in the downlink (DL), and 86.4 Mbit/s for 1×2 antennas in the uplink (UL), and even if optimised for low user mobility (0–15 km/h), it can support higher speed, up to 350 km/h, despite being at lower data rates. In 2011, the specification of LTE Release 10, also called LTE-Advanced, was finalized as a significant improvement of the LTE system and labelled as a fourth generation mobile cellular system (4G). 3GPP has progressively enlarged the initial LTE scope, by specifying features needed for new services and by enriching the possible deployment architectures. Enhancements were added to better support Machine-Type Communications (MTC) and address public safety (mission critical) service requirements. This trend will continue with future evolutions, with 5G intending to address those different sectors from its infancy.

3   3GPP LTE System for Railway

The 3GPP LTE system is based on multi-carrier modulations, Orthogonal Frequency Division Multiplexing (OFDM) in DL and DFT-spread OFDM (DFT-s-OFDM) in UL, which provide flexibility in operating bandwidth [7]. Bandwidths of 1.4, 3, 5, 10, 15 and 20 MHz have been specified up to now and the specifications are written in such a way that any new bandwidth between 1.4 MHz and 20 MHz can be easily added in the specifications. The bandwidth currently allocated to the train radio telecommunication system in Europe is at most 7 MHz, namely 4 MHz around 900 MHz (UIC band) in all European countries, plus an additional 3-MHz bandwidth (E-UIC band) currently available in some countries only. The LTE system can be adapted in order to allow deployments in the complete 7-MHz bandwidth. However, this would require some LTE specification effort in order to define new spectrum masks and radio frequency requirements. Furthermore, the LTE chips for railway would be specific and their price would not benefit from economies of scale. Another option is to stick to already specified bandwidths of 1.4, 3 or 5 MHz. Since the E-UIC band could be subject to interference from Short Range Devices (SRDs), it is expected that part of the 3 MHz will not actually be usable for railways. Hence, an LTE system for railways could operate on the 4 MHz of the UIC band plus 1 MHz of the E-UIC band, for a total of 5 MHz. This latter approach is chosen in this paper. Alternatively, a 3-MHz bandwidth can be used in countries where only the UIC band is available for railway and the 1.4-MHz band when the railway operator wants to make the LTE system coexist with GSM-R during the migration phase, which is expected to last 10 years.

In order to achieve high spectral efficiency whatever the channel conditions and variations, LTE system offers a large panel of specified multi-antenna (MIMO) schemes, including closed-loop multi-stream linear precoding, open-loop multi-stream linear precoding and single-stream transmit diversity schemes [7]. Due to the high train velocity, we focus here on the latter schemes, which are the most robust ones. In LTE DL, the transmit diversity scheme with two transmit antennas is the Alamouti Space Frequency Block Code (SFBC) applied on two adjacent sub-carriers as depicted in Fig. 1. The scheme with four transmit antennas is a combination of Alamouti SFBC and Frequency Switched Transmit Diversity (FSTD) on four adjacent sub-carriers as depicted in Fig. 2 [7]. These two schemes can achieve a spatial diversity of 2 and 4, respectively. With N_R receive antennas, the achievable spatial diversity is multiplied by N_R. In UL, in order to preserve low complexity at the terminal (UE for User Equipment) and good peak-to-average power ratio properties of SC-FDMA, LTE Release 8, which we focus on, only includes closed-loop transmit antenna switching. Due to train mobility resulting in strong channel state information aging, a closed-loop scheme is not feasible. Thus, we focus here on single-antenna SIMO transmission and rely on the base station (BS) receive antennas to obtain a diversity gain.

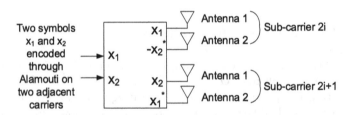

Fig. 1. Downlink LTE Alamouti SFBC transmit diversity scheme with 2 transmit antennas.

4 System Level Evaluation

Link level simulations allow to compute the bit error rate and packet error rate (PER) of a transmission scheme, including detailed simulation of modulation and coding, MIMO scheme, channel estimation, small-scale fading effects and additive white Gaussian noise. However, they do not include any effect of large-scale fading, i.e., distance-dependent pathloss and shadowing. Furthermore, in a cellular system, inter-cell interference has a strong impact on system performance. It depends on large-scale propagation from neighbouring cells and signals transmitted in these cells. Since keeping the same level of details as in link level simulations for a multi-cell system level simulation would result in too much computation effort, computation is reduced by splitting the evaluation in two steps:

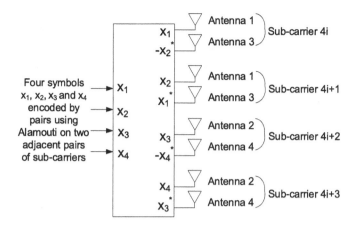

Fig. 2. Downlink LTE Alamouti FSTD-SFBC transmit diversity scheme with 4 transmit antennas.

– Step 1: Link level evaluation
   1. Computation of the PER vs. Signal to Interference plus Noise Ratio (SINR) for transmission schemes (modulation, coding rate, MIMO scheme) with different spectral efficiencies S thanks to a link-level simulation (interference is assumed AWGN) leading to results as shown in Fig. 3
   2. For each scheme and each SINR, computation of the resulting spectral efficiency taking PER into account as $S_{res} = S \times (1 - \text{PER})$
   3. For each SINR, storage of the maximum resulting spectral efficiency (or throughput as shown in Fig. 4) among all schemes as a result of ideal link adaptation
– Step 2: System level evaluation
   1. For many drops of UEs and large-scale channel realizations, computation of SINR for each UE
   2. From all the drops, computation of the Cumulative Density Function (CDF) of the spectral efficiency or throughput by using the obtained SINR as input in the look-up table

System-level simulations are useful to compute the cell average spectral efficiency or the cell-edge throughput (e.g., the 5%-ile throughput, i.e., the maximum throughput among the 5% of UEs with worst SINR). This is particularly important in the frequency reuse 1 LTE deployments which are interference limited, i.e., in which the noise level becomes negligible compared to the interference level.

For evaluating LTE as train radio communication system, we keep the same inter-BS distance as in a typical GSM-R deployment, i.e., 6 km [8], as depicted in Fig. 5. The intention is to be able to reuse GSM-R masts in order to limit the migration cost. In addition to BS deployment, the location of UEs, i.e., trains, strongly impacts the system performance. We evaluate a worst-case train load

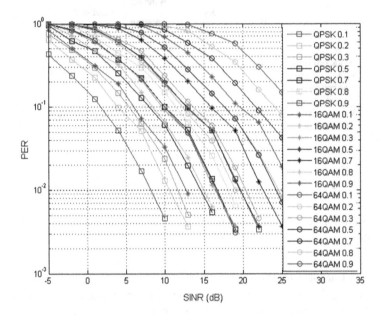

Fig. 3. PER for various downlink transmission schemes (modulation, coding rate) with 4×2 MIMO at $350\,\mathrm{km/h}$ (NLoS RMa channel).

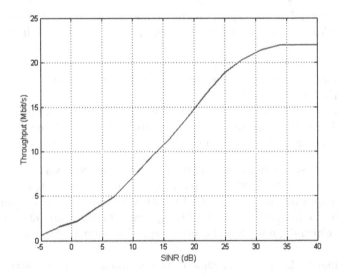

Fig. 4. Maximum resulting throughput among various downlink transmission schemes with 4×2 MIMO at $350\,\mathrm{km/h}$ (NLoS RMa channel).

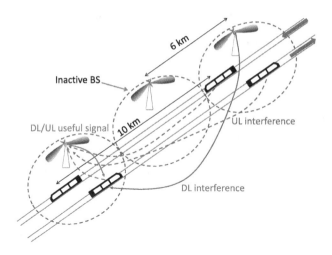

Fig. 5. Railway deployment example.

scenario, in which the train traffic is maximized. Trains move in two opposite directions and trains moving in the same direction are 10 km apart, 10 km being seen as a minimum distance between high speed trains [9]. The distance between two trains in opposite directions is a random value uniformly distributed between 0 and 5 km. A BS is active and generates interference on the downlink signal received at a UE only if there is at least one train located in the cell served by the BS, as depicted in Fig. 5. Likewise, trains moving in both directions and located in neighbouring cells generate interference on the UL signal received at a BS. A worst-case interference level is assumed: all active cells are fully loaded in both UL and DL, i.e., transmission occurs in the whole bandwidth.

The strengths of UE useful signal and interference depend on antenna patterns at the BS and UE and on propagation conditions between the UE and BSs. In the system level evaluation, antenna patterns are taken into account together with BS down-tilt. We use directional antennas at the base station (10° aperture horizontally, 15° vertically), which is suitable in the straight railroad we simulate. At the UE, we simulate an omni-directional antenna.

For the propagation channel, we use the Rural Macro (RMa) channel model as described by ITU for link-level and system-level IMT-Advanced evaluations [10]. This channel model is defined for Line-of-Sight (LoS) and Non-Line-of-Sight (NLoS) and the probability to be in LoS for a UE located at a distance d from a BS is described as

$$p_{LoS} = \exp\left(-\frac{d-10}{1000}\right) \quad \text{where } d \text{ is in meters.}$$

As the train radio telecommunication system will deliver mission-critical services, reliability of the system at any location on the railway is crucial. In order to evaluate this reliability, we compute the throughput CDF at any point of

Table 1. Deployment scenario.

Carrier frequency (DL/UL)	922.5/877.5 MHz
Cell radius	3 km
Train density	2 trains per 10 km
Physical layer	3GPP LTE 5 MHz [7]
Transmit BS/UE max power	46/36 dBm
Transmit UE power control	Full compensation
BS/UE antenna gain	14/0 dB
BS directional antenna pattern	Parabolic in dB scale as MBS in [11] Horizontal Beamwidth: 10° Vertical beamwidth: 15° Vertical Tilt: 20°
Channel estimation	Frequency-domain Wiener and time interpolation
BS/UE antenna gain	14/0 dB
Link channel model, clustered delay lines	ITU-R RMa LoS, KRice = 6 dB, 11 clusters ITU-R RMa NLoS, 10 clusters
Pathloss model	ITU-R RMa LoS & NLoS
Shadowing standard deviation (dB)	4 or 6 dB in LoS, 8 dB in NLoS

the railway, which does not only provide geographical information on the average throughput but also on the 5%-ile throughput. The latter measure is much stricter than the cell-edge throughput computed in 3GPP, which is the cell 5%-ile throughput taken over the whole cell. Here, the 5%-ile throughput is computed for each position and can become very low for trains located at the border between two cells.

Table 1 presents the details of the deployment scenario. The carrier frequency is chosen in order for the system to be located accross the UIC and E-UIC bands. Full compensation is used as UE power control, i.e., the propagation attenuation on the useful signal is compensated regardless of the interference generated on neighbouring cells. This compensation is limited by the UE maximum transmit power.

5   Performance Evaluation

Evaluations are run with 2000 drops. Figure 6 shows the downlink throughput obtained along the line within a cell of radius 3 km with a 4×2 MIMO scheme, at 500 km/h. Due to inter-cell interference, the 5%-ile throughput drops from 19.3 Mbit/s at the cell center down to 2.2 Mbit/s at the cell edge. The inter-cell interference impact is mitigated by the 20° down-tilt at BS. With 0° down-tilt, the 5%-ile throughput drops to 0 at only 1-km distance. This huge interference level can be also mitigated by performing reuse 4 transmission. However, only 3.3 Mbits/s 5%-ile throughput can be achieved at cell-edge and the cell-center 5%-ile throughput is divided by 4 because only a fourth of the available bandwidth is used in each cell. Figure 7 shows similar performance behaviour in uplink, with 1×4 SIMO.

Tables 2 and 3 present a summary of LTE performance for different speeds and MIMO schemes, in DL and UL respectively. Using more antennas slightly increases the throughput at cell center and along the line, except at 500 km/h in downlink. Indeed, the pilot density is reduced for the two additional antennas compared to the 2-transmit-antenna case. Thus, the 4×2 MIMO scheme suffers from poorer channel estimation at high speed. Cell-edge performance is also slightly decreased due to higher pilot overhead. The results also confirm that the LTE system can cope with high speeds up to 500 km/h in railway environment

Table 2. Summary of DL LTE throughput results.

Train velocity (km/h)	MIMO	Cell-center 5%-ile throughput (Mbit/s)	Cell-edge 5%-ile throughput (Mbit/s)	Whole-cell average throughput (Mbit/s)	Whole-cell 5%-ile throughput (Mbit/s)
30	2×2	21.7	2.2	16.9	4.2
30	4×2	21.9	2.2	17.3	4.6
350	2×2	21.6	2.1	16.9	4.3
350	4×2	22.0	2.2	17.0	4.6
500	2×2	21.6	2.1	16.8	4.2
500	4×2	19.3	2.2	15.1	4.5

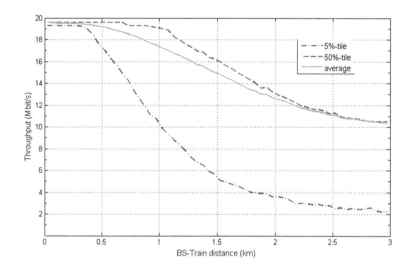

Fig. 6. Downlink throughput with 4×2 MIMO at 500 km/h.

Table 3. Summary of UL LTE throughput results.

Train velocity (km/h)	MIMO	Cell-center 5%-ile throughput (Mbit/s)	Cell-edge 5%-ile throughput (kbit/s)	Whole-cell average throughput (Mbit/s)	Whole-cell 5%-ile throughput (Mbit/s)
30	1×2	18	150	12.7	2.0
30	1×4	18	300	13.7	2.9
350	1×2	17.9	100	12.5	1.9
350	1×4	18	240	13.5	2.7
500	1×2	15.5	100	11.0	1.8
500	1×4	15.9	220	11.9	2.7

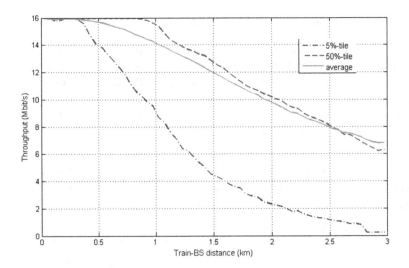

Fig. 7. Uplink throughput with 1×4 SIMO at $500\,\mathrm{km/h}$.

and that throughput is not significantly degraded by such high speeds. However, 5%-ile throughput remains very low at cell edge, especially in uplink, even if it achieves a few Mbits/s when computed over the whole cell.

6 Conclusion

System-level evaluation of the LTE mobile system in a railway environment have shown that LTE can cope with high train speed. However, if railway operators target a guaranteed minimum throughput 95% of the time at any location of the railway, the guaranteed throughput at the border between two cells drops to a few hundreds of kbit/s in uplink, which might not be enough, e.g., to deliver CCTV services, for which the required throughput per camera ranges between a few hundreds of kbit/s for low quality and a few Mbit/s for high quality. Especially, the latter high quality may be needed for look-ahead control. Interference coordination might be a solution, as hard frequency reuse strongly degrades the cell-center throughput. Another solution would be to investigate the next generation of mobile cellular systems, namely the 5G system under specification in 3GPP.

References

1. Bonneville, H., Brunel, L., Mottier, D.: Standardisation roadmap for next train radio telecommunication systems. In: Communication Technologies for Vehicles - 10th International Workshop, Nets4Cars/Nets4Trains/Nets4Aircraft 2016, San Sebastián, Spain, 6–7 June, 2016, Proceedings, pp. 51–61 (2016)
2. UIC. Railway Mobile Communication System User Requirement. International Railway Union, Technical report, October 2010
3. ERA. Evolution of GSM-R - Final Report. European Railway Agency, Technical report, ERA/2014/04/ERTMS/OP, April 2015
4. 3GPP. Study on Future Railway Mobile Communication System; V0.3.0. 3rd Generation Partnership Project (3GPP), 3GPP Work Item Description SP-160903, January 2017
5. Study on Future Railway Mobile Communication System; Stage 1, 3rd Generation Partnership Project (3GPP), TR 22.889, December 2016
6. ETSI. GSM-R networks evolution. System Reference document (SRDoc), TR 103.333, December 2016
7. 3GPP. Evolved Universal Terrestrial Radio Access (E-UTRA); Physical Channels and Modulation. 3rd Generation Partnership Project (3GPP), TS 36.211, December 2012
8. Guo, H., Wu, H., Zhang, Y.: GSM-R network planning for high speed railway. In: IET 3rd International Conference on Wireless, Mobile and Multimedia Networks (ICWMNN 2010), pp. 10–13, September 2010
9. Connor, P.: Rules for high speed line capacity. In: Railway Technical Web Pages, August 2011
10. ITU-R. Guidelines for evaluation of radio interface technologies for IMT-Advanced. International Telecommunication Union - Radiocommunication, TR M.2135-1, December 2009
11. 3GPP. Spatial channel model for Multiple Input Multiple Output (MIMO) simulations. 3rd Generation Partnership Project (3GPP), TR 25.996, September 2014

ITS-G5 Channel Models for High Speed Train-to-Train Communication

Paul Unterhuber[✉], Mohammad Soliman, and Andreas Lehner

Institute of Communications and Navigation, German Aerospace Center (DLR),
Oberpfaffenhofen, 82234 Wessling, Germany
paul.unterhuber@dlr.de

Abstract. Train-to-train communication will be the key technology for future railway operation. An increase of safety and efficiency can be achieved by exchanging data between trains via ad hoc networks. For vehicle-to-vehicle communication the European standard is intelligent transport systems (ITS-G5). The usage of this standard for railways is hardly investigated. We investigate the performance of ITS-G5 for train-to- train communication at high speed conditions. ITS-G5 units were installed on two high speed trains and train-to-train (T2T) measurements were performed between Naples and Rome during four nights to cover different maneuvers. We present the analysis of the measurements data and resulting path loss models for tunnel and open field environments.

Keywords: T2T · Electronic coupling · ITS-G5 · Channel model · NGT

1 Introduction

On the path towards autonomous driving trains, electronic coupling is seen as the door opener application. Electronic coupled trains are connected with a wireless communication link, but without a mechanical coupler [1]. For this application, different T2T communication links are envisaged. We use three categories: short, mid and long range communication links. On short range of several hundred meters, ultra reliability and low latency are required to support precise distance control of the trains over wireless train control management system. For mid range communication between two trains, e.g. up to 2 km, a robust data link needs to be established which allows for a safe approach. Therefore, safety related information like movement information need to be exchanged with medium data rates under certain delay and error constraints. For long distances a terrestrial trunked radio (TETRA) based system could be used to ensure links up to a few tens of kilometers with low data rates as proposed in [2].

So far T2T is hardly investigated compared to train-to-ground communications. T2T channel models covering high speed scenarios and frequencies above 1 GHz are not discussed in literature. The necessity of investigations on short and mid range T2T links and related channel models is pointed out in [3]. A technology transfer from vehicular applications developed for road traffic like ITS-G5 to high speed trains in the railway domain needs to be verified.

© Springer International Publishing AG 2017
A. Pirovano et al. (Eds.): Nets4Cars/Nets4Trains/Nets4Aircraft 2017, LNCS 10222, pp. 72–83, 2017.
DOI: 10.1007/978-3-319-56880-5_8

Based on previous measurements with commuter trains at speeds up to 140 km/h as presented in [4], we have set up an ITS-G5 system in two high speed trains (HSTs). This measurement campaign was performed in Italy in 2016 and is described in detail in [5]. In this paper we present an extended evaluation of the ITS-G5 link measurements in high speed railway (HSR) environments and deriving path loss channel models for certain railway environments.

2   Measurement Campaign

A comprehensive four days measurement campaign was planned and performed on the 220 km long HSR track between Naples and Rome in Italy. One night was used for intra-consist communication measurements (published in [6]) with one Trenitalia Frecciarossa ETR 500 HST [7] as shown in Fig. 1. In the following three nights, different T2T measurements with two of those HSTs were performed. Different measurement systems were installed. Next to an ITS-G5 communication link, a TETRA based communication system was installed and tested under high speed conditions as presented in [8]. The DLR RUSK channel sounder was used for intra-consist and T2T measurements at 5.2 GHz. For the movement tracking of both trains, global navigation satellite system (GNSS) receivers and inertial measurement units (IMUs) were mounted in the trains. More details on the campaign and the installed equipment can be found in [5].

2.1   ITS-G5 Equipment and Setup

Both HSTs were equipped with ITS-G5 Cohda Wireless MK-5 modules. The on board unit of Train 07 was set up as transmitter (Tx) and the unit of Train 28 as receiver (Rx). The general settings are listed in Table 1. The settings were chosen to ensure the most robust link. The radios were set up for the control channel 180 at 5.9 GHz with a bandwidth of 10 MHz. The output power of the Tx ITS-G5 module was set to the maximum of 23 dBm. On the Tx side, an additional amplifier was used to achieve in combination with the installed antenna an equivalent isotropically radiated power (EIRP) of 31 dBm. The data rate was set to 3 Mbit/s with BPSK modulation at a coding rate of 1/2. The packet length was 400 Byte with a repetition rate of 100 Hz.

To fulfill the safety regulations for railways, railway certified antennas were used. Huber+Suhner SWA-0859/360/4/0/DFRX30_2 omni-directional antennas were installed on the first coach after the locomotive of each train. These antennas support multiple bands up to 6 GHz and offer an integrated GNSS antenna.

The Cohda MK-5 modules offer a dual transceiver radio. For these measurements, only radio A was activated and connected to the measurement antenna. The internal GNSS receiver was used to log the train positions for each received signal strength indication (RSSI) measurement.

The Tx data included a header with a sequential packet number, the movement information of the Train 07 and dummy payload data. The movement

Table 1. Cohda MK5 radio settings

Channel	180
Carrier frequency	5.9 GHz
Bandwidth	10 MHz
EIRP	31 dBm
Data rate	3 Mbit/s
Modulation	BPSK
Coding rate	1/2
Packet length	400 Byte
Repetition rate	100 Hz

information of Train 07 and Train 28 and the RSSI measurements were stored together with the GPS time stamp on the Cohda module at Train 28.

2.2 Environment and Scenarios

The measurement campaign was performed at night from midnight to 5 am out of scheduled operation time in spring 2016. The environment along the track varies from urban and suburban areas around Naples to rural areas before arriving in Rome. A map of the HSR track is plotted in Fig. 2 and marked in red. Open field, forest, hilly sections and tunnels alternate in the rural area.

Nowadays, typical HST maneuvers include mainly crossing and sometimes overtaking. An overtake maneuver is comparable with an approaching maneuver for electronic coupling. Therefore, the overtaking maneuver was specially performed in all characteristic environments for different speeds. The low speed measurements were performed at 50 km/h and the high speed at 250 km/h average absolute velocity. The combination of environments and maneuvers with different velocities lead to the measurement scenarios listed in Table 2. For all measurements, the trains were driving on different parallel tracks.

For the analysis in Sect. 3 we are focusing on open field and tunnels at high speed. We present one overtake maneuver for each environment.

Table 2. Measurement scenarios

	Slow	Fast
(Sub-) urban	x	
Rural	x	x
Tunnel		x

Fig. 1. Trenitalia Frecciarossa ETR 500 HST.

Fig. 2. HSR track Naples-Rome. Image by Google, Map Data 2016 NOAA, U.S. Navy, NGA, GEBCO Image Landsat (2015). (Color figure online)

3   Data Analysis

3.1   Path Loss Models

Two path loss models were chosen to estimate the losses in different environments. The free-space path loss equation

$$FSPL(d) = 20 \cdot log_{10}(\frac{4\pi d \cdot f}{c}) \tag{1}$$

was used as reference. d represents the distance between Tx and Rx antenna, f the carrier frequency and c the speed of light.

The log-distance path loss model was used to model line of sight (LOS) and non LOS conditions. In addition to a reference path loss at a distance $d_0 = 1\,m$, a relation of the actual distance d and d_0 times a path loss exponent n is added. The power variations due to shadowing and multi path effects are modeled as normal distributed vector $\chi_\sigma \sim \mathcal{N}(0, \sigma)$.

$$PL(d) = FSPL(d_0) + 10 \cdot n \cdot log_{10}(\frac{d}{d_0}) + \chi_\sigma \tag{2}$$

3.2   Scenarios

Figures 3, 4, 5, 6, 7, 8, and 9 show the measurement analysis in open field and tunnel environment. In general, the received power, the distance and speed of the trains over time are plotted in Figs. 3 and 7. The received power and the fitted path loss of the log-distance model are plotted in Figs. 4 and 8. Figures 5 and 9 show the probability density of the fading effects in case of the log-distance model.

Open Field: First, we present an approaching maneuver in a rural environment. As shown in Fig. 3, the Tx Train 07 is between 300 m and 400 m in front of the Rx Train 28. Both trains are accelerating from 100 km/h to 250 km/h. In this phase of the maneuver both trains could be seen as one electronically coupled consist. Up from 200 s the Rx is accelerating up to 300 km/h and reducing the gap, finally overtaking the Tx train. Out of the top chart of Fig. 3 we can derive, that fades are less related to the speed than to the distance between Tx and Rx.

In Fig. 4 the measured received power is plotted over distance in green. The related FSPL model and log-distance model are plotted in red and black. As already mentioned before, up from a distance of 200 m deeper fades can be observed; this is caused by a higher probability of non LOS components. Even in open field environment, catenary, pylons or the signaling system can cause multi path components (MPCs). More information on multi paths in railway environments can be found in [3,5]. As expected for open field there is high probability for LOS. Therefore, FSPL model fits quite well to the measured received power. At higher distances the log-distance model with a path loss exponent of $n = 2.1$ fits better than the FSPL model.

The shadowing was analyzed as well and fitted to a normal distribution as shown in Fig. 5. The log-distance model parameters are listed in Table 3.

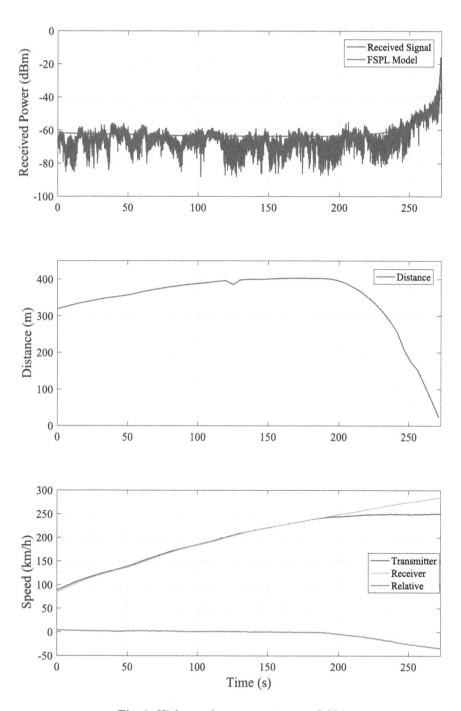

Fig. 3. High speed maneuver in open field

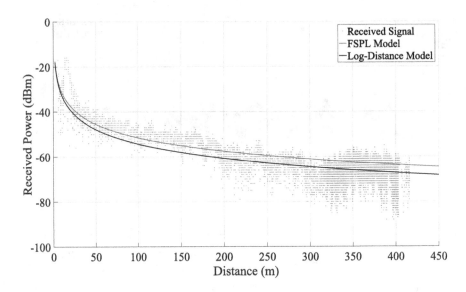

Fig. 4. Path loss model for open field (Color figure online)

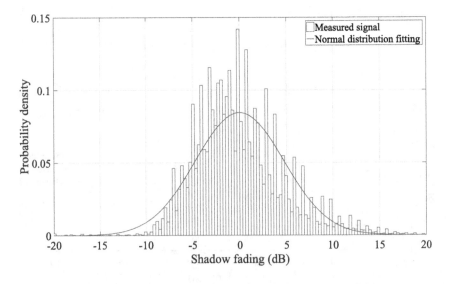

Fig. 5. Probability density of shadow fading for open field

Fig. 6. Track for tunnel section, blue indicates tunnels. Image by Google, Map Data 2016 NOAA, U.S. Navy, GEBCO Image Landsat (2015). (Color figure online)

Tunnels: The second maneuver is a departure and approaching in a hilly environment with several consecutive tunnels. In Fig. 6 the tunnels are marked in blue; the trains are driving from right to left side of the figure. Hence, at least one train was always in a tunnel and several times, Tx and Rx were in the same tunnel or in two consecutive tunnels. This is illustrated with colored bars in the top chart of Fig. 7.

The analysis of the maneuver starts at 0 s when Rx is overtaking Tx with a speed of 140 km/h and accelerates to 200 km/h. Rx runs ahead till 165 s up to a maximum distance of 2.1 km. Tx is accelerating from 50 km/h to 270 km/h and catching up to Rx at 275 s.

While both trains were driving through the longest tunnel marked in orange, the distance was above 2 km. Up from around 250 s, both trains were in a same tunnel again (brown tunnel). For both events, the received power was 18 dB above the FSPL model. This gain is caused by a wave guiding effect inside the tunnels. Around 50 s and 70 s similar effects can be observed with a gain of 15 dB. In these sections the trains were in different, but very close tunnels.

For constellations with large areas of open field between different tunnels (e.g. 90–120 s or 210–240 s), only one train was inside a tunnel. In these sections the received power is 15–20 dB beneath the FSPL model, because diffraction at the tunnel entry causes extra loss [2].

Figure 8 shows the received power over distance for two cases. At the first and general case at least on train is in a tunnel (marked in green). This case is modeled by the free-space path loss (FSPL) model in red. Second case marked with blue dots, both trains are in the same or very close tunnels. This case is modeled by the log-distance model in black. For both cases, strong wave guiding effects can be observed for distances beneath 500 m and above 2000 m. If at least one train is in a tunnel, deep fades can be observed for distances above 500 m.

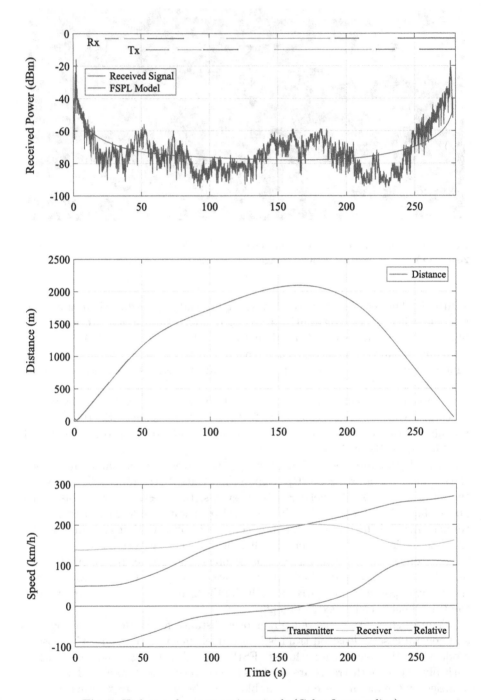

Fig. 7. High speed maneuver in tunnels (Color figure online)

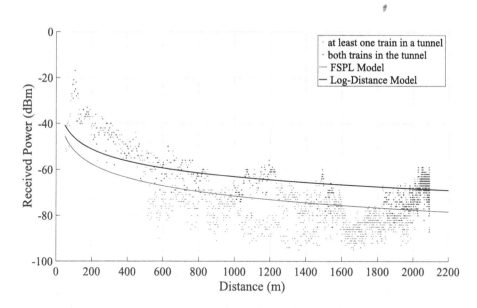

Fig. 8. Path loss model for tunnel environment (Color figure online)

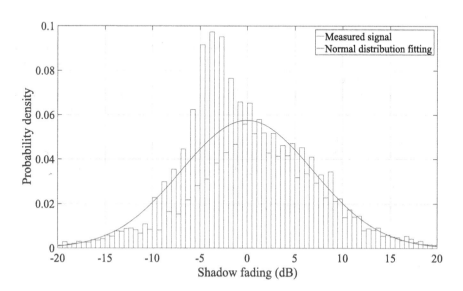

Fig. 9. Probability density of shadow fading for both trains in a tunnel (Color figure online)

Table 3. Log-distance model parameters

	$PL(d_0)$ dBm	n	σ dB
Open field	47.8	2.1	4.72
Tunnels	47.8	1.72	6.93

The probability density of the shadowing is plotted in blue in Fig. 9 for the case where both trains are inside a tunnel. A normal distribution is fitted to the measured signal with the parameters listed in Table 3.

4 Conclusion

In this paper we presented an analysis of ITS-G5 as T2T link under HSR conditions. The performance at open field environment and tunnels at high speed were investigated in detail. For both environments, the received power was measured while performing overtaking maneuvers with two HSTs.

In detail, deep fades can be observed for link distances above 200 m in open field and above 500 m in tunnels. If Tx and Rx are in the same tunnel or close tunnels, a wave guide effect with a maximum gain of 18 dB can be observed. For mixed environments with tunnels and open field, alternating strong fading effects and shadowing affect the link significantly. Nevertheless, stable links could be achieved for distances up to 2 km. The high speed ($\geq$200 km/h) has no significant effect on the data transmission.

For both environments, log-distance models were derived and the parameters presented. In comparison to car-to-car communication, larger communication ranges can be achieved by similar data rates. Furthermore, the dynamic of trains is smaller than for road vehicles. As already presented in [4] the update delay is sufficient for electronic coupling application. Hence, the ITS-G5 standard is suitable for mid range communication for electronic coupling applications.

Acknowledgement. The authors are thankful for the support of the European Commission through the Roll2Rail project [9], one of the lighthouse projects of Shift2Rail [10] within the Horizon 2020 program. The Roll2Rail project has received funding from the European Union's Horizon 2020 research and innovation program under Grant Agreement no. 636032.

References

1. Winter, J., Lehner, A., Polisky, E.: Electronic coupling of next generation trains. In: 3rd International Conference on Railway Technology: Research, Development and Maintenance, Cagliari. Civil-Comp Press (2016)
2. Lehner, A., García, C.R., Strang, T.: On the performance of TETRA DMO short data service in railway VANETs. Wirel. Pers. Commun. **69**(4), 1647–1669 (2013)

3. Unterhuber, P., Pfletschinger, S., Sand, S., et al.: A survey of channel measurements and models for current and future railway communication systems. Mob. Inf. Syst. **2016**, 1–14 (2016). Article ID 7308604. doi:10.1155/2016/7308604

4. Unterhuber, P., Lehner, A., de Ponte Müller, F.: Measurement and analysis of ITS-G5 in railway environments. In: Communication Technologies for Vehicles, San Sebastian, pp. 62–73 (2016)

5. Unterhuber, P., Soliman, M., Gera, D.: Wide band propagation in train-to-train scenarios - measurement campaign and first results. In: 11th European Conference on Antennas and Propagation, Paris. IEEE (2017)

6. Soliman, M., Unterhuber, P., Gera, D.: First analysis of inside train communication with ITS-G5 measurement data. In: Thirteenth International Symposium on Wireless Communication Systems, Poznan. IEEE (2016)

7. Trenitalia ETR 500 (2017). www.trenitalia.it

8. Lehner, A., Strang, T., Unterhuber, P.: Train-to-train at 450 MHz. In: 11th European Conference on Antennas and Propagation, Paris. IEEE (2017)

9. Roll2Rrail (2017). www.roll2rail.eu

10. Shift2Rail (2017). www.shift2rail.org

On-Board Electromagnetic Interference Field-Test and Evaluation of a Non-electrified Railway Regional Line

Jaizki Mendizabal[(✉)], Gorka De Miguel, Julen Uranga, Beatriz Sedano, Jon Goya, and Iñigo Adin

CEIT and Tecnun (University of Navarra), Manuel de Lardizabal 15,
20018 San Sebastián, Spain
{jmendizabal,gdemiguel,juranga,bsedano,jgoya,iadin}@ceit.es

Abstract. In order to assess the performance of the wireless communication systems, a railway line is characterised through the identification of electromagnetic interferences (EMI). The aim of this paper is to show the strategy to identify EMI on field as well as the results obtained. First, the need of the analysis and the objectives of the measurement campaign in a non-electrified Italian Regional Railway line between Caligari and San Gavino are shown. After that, the measurement setup developed for the tests is described. Then, the description of the measurement campaign carried out is exposed. Finally, the measurement results are presented. The results show that the frequency bands of GSM, UMTS and Italian 4G are in the frequency ranges where the highest powered signal (around 800 MHz–900 MHz, 1.8 GHz and 1.9 GHz), on the other hand GPS L1 and Galileo E1 frequency band is not impacted by any kind of interference signal.

Keywords: Electromagnetic interferences (EMI) · Field testing · Railway · Wireless communication · Regional line

1 Introduction

The increasing number of electronics and communication equipment installed on the trains and infrastructure makes it necessary to characterise the electromagnetic interferences (EMI) environment in the railway lines. The impact of the environment still is being studied for different railway communications and signalling systems, such as ERTMS [1, 2] or some of its constituents [3]. Depending on the different types of railway infrastructure such as electrified lines, double track lines, etc. the electromagnetic environment differs. For example, special attention has been given to the interferences found in the antennas installed on the roof of the train in electrified lines with catenary and pantograph [4–6].

The environment affects the performance of the equipment installed in the operation. Therefore, the electromagnetic environment should be taken into account in the development phase and validation phase of the equipment. These phases require to have a characterised electromagnetic environment with the aim of foresee the performance of the wireless communication systems installed on-board and in the infrastructure.

© Springer International Publishing AG 2017
A. Pirovano et al. (Eds.): Nets4Cars/Nets4Trains/Nets4Aircraft 2017, LNCS 10222, pp. 84–96, 2017.
DOI: 10.1007/978-3-319-56880-5_9

Previous works have been done to define the electromagnetic environment and employ it in the development and validation phase such as the study of the ETCS's (European Train Control System) Eurobalise and Balise Transmission Module (BTM) [7], methodologies for system development including EMC (ElectroMagnetic Compatibility) analysis [8] and even including mitigation techniques. This will also lead to the certification validation in the laboratory [9] of different systems such as BTM [10]. Moreover, EMC standards should be updated including new threats are found in the railway environment [11].

This paper outlines the objectives of the EMI measurement campaign and the main outputs that can be extracted from it. The objective of the measurement campaign performed by CEIT was to characterise the railway pilot line environment in terms of EMI. To acquire EMI information, tests in both static and dynamic modes have been carried out in order to analyse the performance over the railway site.

This paper is structured as follows.

- Section 2 introduces the equipment used during this activity.
- Section 3 explains corresponding test procedure.
- Section 4 describes the measurement campaign.
- Section 5 shows the results obtained.
- Finally Sect. 6 presents conclusions.

2 Measurement Equipment

The set of equipment used to carry out the data collection in the regional railway line is presented and explained in this section. It is composed of several kinds of receivers and antennas. Some of them were already installed on the test locomotive in the pilot line and other were installed ad-hoc for the test-campaign. The test setup and test procedure are first validated and calibrated in the laboratory, before moving to perform the filed tests.

Figure 1 represents the three different chains of the test setup defined for the measurement campaign. The one on the left is responsible to register position, speed and time by means of the GNSS receiver. The one on the middle is in charge of the recording the interferences around the frequency bands under study. The one on the right connected with the modem offers the connection to the GSM and/or UMTS networks.

- The first chain was included with the aim of adding a time and geolocation stamp to the recorded interference.
- The second chain has been designed and implemented to record the interfering signals present in the target frequency bands. This will allow to evaluate their influence in the system under study. To record the interference signals, a high speed digitizer is employed. A script designed in Labview has been used in order to control and command the digitizer including time reference synchronization. The raw interfering signals can be recorded in two different ways: in a continuous way in a given time step or when a trigger happens. In the site measurement campaign both approaches have been used.

- The third chain is helpful for determining the interferences affecting the voice and data communication systems at the trial site during this measurement campaign. The GSM/UMTS modem is the one in charge of the GSM/UMTS traffic recordings. In that case, the modem establishes the communication with the surrounding base stations and the data received is recorded. In this case, the Base Station (BS) connected to the GSM/UMTS modem sends back the following information: Date and Time, Cell Type, Mobile Country Code, Mobile Network Code, Location Area Code, Cell Identification, Received Level and Timing Advance.

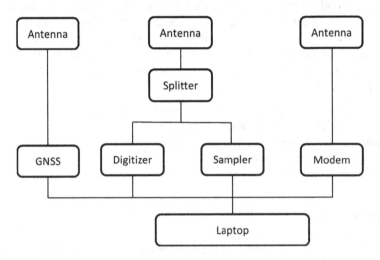

Fig. 1. Test setup to determine interferers and record them

The following equipment will be described in the next subsections.

- Antennae.
- GNSS receiver.
- High Frequency Digitizer.
- Sampler.
- Modem.
- Laptop.

2.1 Antennae

Three antenna already installed on the locomotive (see Fig. 2) have been used in this trial. They can operate in all frequency ranges between 790 MHz and 2700 MHz; in this particular case, they are used for GPS and 2G/3G (communication).

Fig. 2. Antennae on the roof of the locomotive (Courtesy of Ansaldo STS)

2.2 GNSS Receiver

For each GPS time epoch, the observation and navigation information produced by the GNSS receivers with a rate of 5 Hz are stored. Such receivers are complementary to the raw data recording (performed by the high speed digitizer, see next subsection) in order to synchronize and position the events.

The following measurements for GPS L1 have been recorded, at a rate of 5 Hz:

1. UTC time in terms of hours, minutes and seconds.
2. WGS84 Latitude, longitude in degrees and height in meters.
3. Carrier to noise ratio for each available satellite in dB-Hz.
4. Speed.
5. Loss of lock indicator.

2.3 High Frequency Digitizer

The high frequency digitizer used to capture the raw high frequency signals found in the environment of the GPS L1 and Galileo E1 band is a PXI from National Instruments. This is a rugged PC-based platform for measurement and automation systems. Each PXI combines PCI electrical-bus features with the modular, Eurocard packaging of Compact PCI and then adds specialized synchronization buses and key software features. The one used in the Pilot Line characterization with a PXIe-1073 chassis and a PXIe-5162 Digitizer with 1.5 GHz bandwidth, 5 GS/s and 10-Bit.

This digitizer is controlled by a LabView script specifically designed for that measurement campaign, with a synchronization of the UTC time (from GPS) with the laptop time and the integration of other data on the recording (Fig. 3).

Fig. 3. High speed digitizer – PXI

2.4 Sampler

The Acorde ACGNS-L1 E1-FE-v2 is a signal sampler that delivers I/Q data at Intermediate Frequency (IF) and the AGC (Automatic Gain Control) configuration status used at every sample. Both information are given with a rate of 1.5 Hz. This is employed to identify potential interferers with the aim of triggering the software in the laptop (Fig. 4).

Fig. 4. AGC controlled sampler

2.5 GSM/UMTS Modem

The modem presented in Fig. 5 provides simple, flexible and ready-to-use environments for evaluating u-blox LISA-U230 W-CDMA cellular modules, as well as for designing and testing cellular and GNSS applications. This system has both USB and RS232 interfaces for development, testing and tracking. The picture shows a portable antenna, but during this measurement campaign, this has not been used, as the modem has been connected to the GSM/UMTS antenna already installed on-board the locomotive.

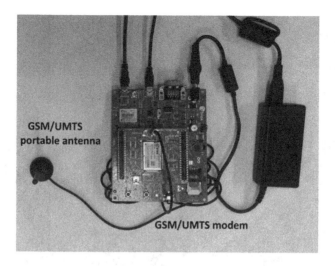

Fig. 5. GSM/UMTS modem setup

2.6 Laptop

Figure 6 presents a picture of the setup installed inside the locomotive during the measurement campaign at the pilot line where the laptop employed can be clearly identified. This picture shows the high speed digitizer part of the test setup to record the EMI. Moreover, all the communication devices, cables, connectors, etc. are inside the box. The block diagram of the complete test setup used here is presented in Fig. 1.

3 Measurement Procedure

This section shows the test procedure to detect unknown blocking scenarios (EMI). At the beginning of every journey, the sampler needs to be switched on in order to obtain the standstill value for that moment and the conditions surrounding. By means of the second chain of the test setup (see Fig. 1) the AGC gain value is employed. For the AGC gain value, a threshold is defined, 3 dB margin for this case[1]. The recording of the data is done every time a significant variation from the standstill conditions have been detected in the signal received. Once connected to the high speed digitiser, by means of the Labview script on the laptop, every time the AGC gain reaches the trigger levels, the high speed digitiser records the raw signals captured at the GPS antenna with the following characteristics and format:

- 5Gsamples/s.
- 1Msample word (equivalent to 200 µs).
- Percentage of backward recording (customized at the Labview script).

---

[1] This value implies that the AGC introduces a gain that is half the needed gain in standard operation.

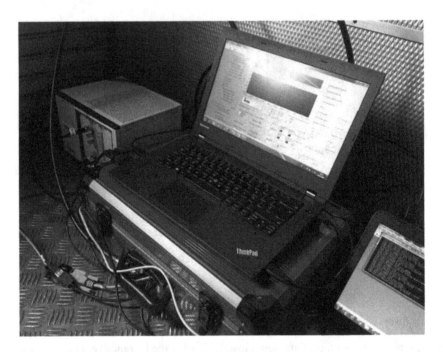

Fig. 6. Picture with the setup in the pilot line

- HWS format (NI proprietary) with a0 and a1 coefficients depending on the amplitude range expected at the input of the high speed digitizer (defined at the Labview script).

The other implementation for that data recording is applied with no triggers. In that case, the signals captured by the antenna are recorded continuously for the entire journey. The number of files that can be saved per second depends on the availability of the communication link (PCI Slot).

The second chain needs to be synchronised to the same time reference by means of the GPS signal. At the start up, the GSM/UMTS observables recording application needs a UTC time provided by the embedded GPS receiver to its module. Once the time is set, the application switches to obtain data. The Base Station connected to the GSM/UMTS modem sends back the following information: Date and Time, Cell Type, Mobile Country Code, Mobile Network Code, Location Area Code, Cell Identification, Received Level and Timing Advance.

4 Measurement Campaign

The objective of measurement campaign performed by CEIT is to characterise the Regional Railway pilot line located in Italy in terms of EMI in the frequency band under study that cover mobile phone telecommunication technologies frequency bands and in the GPS frequency bands. The measurement campaign was performed during five days

Fig. 7. Diesel locomotive ALN 668-3114 from Trenitalia

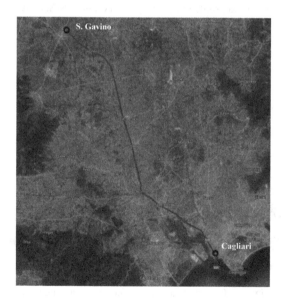

Fig. 8. Sardinia pilot railway site

in the Sardinia pilot railway site, from 26.01.2016 to 29.01.2016. General details of the measurement campaign are (Fig. 7):

- Time frame: from 26.01.2016 to 29.01.2016.
- Railway line: Cagliari – San Gavino.
- Dynamic vehicle: Diesel locomotive ALN 668-3114 from Trenitalia.

During this data collection, two types of measurements were done (Fig. 8):

- Dynamic: Three return ones because it was a round trip – 9:00–11:00 CET, 13:00–15:00 CET and 16:00–18:00 CET approx.
- Static: at S. Gavino and at Cagliari locations with different durations depending on the train stop with a duration of approx. 3–5 min.

Figure 9 presents the results of one of the journeys, in this case from Cagliari to San Gavino, on the 27/01/2016. Figure 10 shows the speed profile with 5 stops during the operation between Cagliari and San Gavino. The recording of the data started before the starting of the train in both cases. The dynamic test has used commercial operation of the train and consequently, the stops and the operative speed assigned to this train and this line have been respected (Fig. 11).

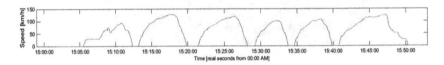

Fig. 9. Speed profile of a journey from Cagliari to San Gavino

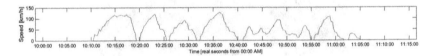

Fig. 10. Speed profile of a journey from San Gavino to Cagliari

Fig. 11. General landscape in Sardinia pilot site [12]

The pilot line where the measurement campaign was performed is placed in an open-view-sky area; rural environment with some industrial facilities not so high and several bridges. Next figures show the environment in the pilot test site (Fig. 12).

Fig. 12. General obstacles in Sardinia pilot site [12]

5 Results

Firstly, in a preliminary inspection, the track from Cagliari to San Gavino seemed to show a good clearance from the interference sources point of view. Actually, all the journeys have obtained similar conclusions once the post-processing of the data has been completed.

The test setup and test procedure presented have been applied during the journeys all along the test pilot site. Figure 13 shows the time-based representation of some of the most powerful signals (interferers), in dBm, extracted from the complete set of signals recorded in the test campaign.

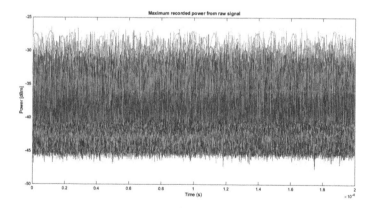

Fig. 13. Interface signals maximum power recorder

Figure 14 shows a zoom of where some of the most significant signals are plotted. Some of these signals start during the recording, which means that this kind of communication could be not permanent. That point is consistent with the observation of CEIT in other research project on similar matter [13] from measurements of another railway line.

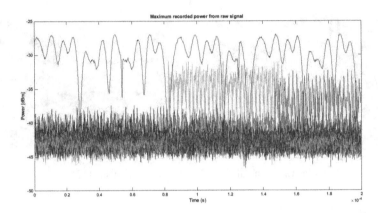

Fig. 14. Significant transients of the interference signals maximum power recorded

Figure 15 shows a merged representation of the time-frequency analysis done to the raw transients extracted from the continuous recording into one single plot. It is clear that the GPS L1 and Galileo E1 band is not impacted by any kind of interference signal. The GSM, the UMTS and the Italian 4G bands are the ones showing the higher powered signal at the antenna connected to the high speed digitizer (around 800 MHz–900 MHz, 1.8 GHz and 1.9 GHz), but the power level should to impact the quality of the communication. Also, mention that the 1.25 GHz frequency is also significant in that plot due to the downsampling operation of the digitizer.

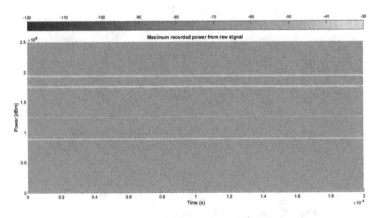

Fig. 15. Time-Frequency plot of the continuous recording of signals

6   Conclusions

The test setup and a test measurement procedure defined showed that they are suitable to detect EMI on-board a train in an operational line, in this case the Regional Railway pilot line between Cagliari and San Gavino in Italy. The measurements campaign carried out was enough to address the conclusions of the electromagnetic environment of the railway line under study.

As it was expected, the results show that the electromagnetic environment for the non-electric regional railway line does not show any interference that could impact the wireless communications. GPS L1 and Galileo E1frequency band is not impacted by any kind of interference signal. On the other hand, the frequency bands of GSM, UMTS and Italian 4G are in the frequency ranges where the highest powered signal (around 800 MHz–900 MHz, 1.8 GHz and 1.9 GHz).

Future work for CEIT continues in other environments such as electrified lines, urban environments, high speed lines or freight lines where further effects are expected to be found.

Acknowledgements. This research was supported by the ERSAT-EAV project [14] as part of the European H2020 framework of projects funded by the European Commission (EC) and managed by the European GNSS Agency (GSA).

The author want to express especial thanks to our ERSAT-EAV project colleagues from Ansaldo STS, RFI, Trenitalia and ESSP who allowed both measuring campaigns in the project's framework and the use of their infrastructure.

References

1. Adín, I., Mendizabal, J., del Portillo, J.: Impact of electromagnetic environment on reliability assessment for railway signalling systems. In: Railway Safety, Reliability, and Security (2012)
2. Mansson, D., Thottappillil, R., Backstrom, M., Lunden, O.: Vulnerability of European rail traffic management system to radiated intentional EMI. IEEE Trans. Electromagn. Compat. **50**(1), 101–109 (2008)
3. Mendizabal, J., Solas, G., Valdivia, Leonardo J., Miguel, G., Uranga, J., Adin, I.: ETCS's Eurobalise-BTM and Euroloop-LTM airgap noise and interferences review. In: Mendizabal, J., Berbineau, M., Vinel, A., Pfletschinger, S., Bonneville, H., Pirovano, A., Plass, S., Scopigno, R., Aniss, H. (eds.) Nets4Cars/Nets4Trains/Nets4Aircraft 2016. LNCS, vol. 9669, pp. 27–39. Springer, Cham (2016). doi:10.1007/978-3-319-38921-9_4
4. Tellini, B., Macucci, M., Giannetti, R., Antonacci, G.A.: Line-pantograph EMI in railway systems. IEEE Instrum. Meas. Mag. **4**(4), 10–13 (2001)
5. Deniau, V., Fridhi, H., Heddebaut, M., Rioult, J. Rodriguez, J., Adín, I.: Analysis and modelling of the EM interferences produced above a train associated to the contact between the catenary and the pantograph. In: EMC Europe 2013, Brugge, 2–6 Septiembre 2013
6. Fridhi, H., Deniau, V., Ghys, J.P., Heddebaut, M., Rodriguez, J., Adín, I.: Analysis of the coupling path between transient EM interferences produced by the catenary-pantograph contact and on-board railway communication antennas, In: ICEAA 2013, Torino (Italy) 9–13 September 2013
7. Adin, I., Mendizabal, J., Arrizabalaga, S., Alvarado, U., Solas, G., Rodriguez, J.: Rolling stock emission testing methodology assessment for Balise Transmission Module system interoperability. Measurement **77**, 124–131 (2016)
8. del Portillo, J., Mendizabal, J., Adín, I., Melendez, J., de No, J., Alvarado, U.: Functional, Thermal and EMC analysis for a safety critical analogue design applied to a transportation system. In: Simultech 2011 (2011)

9. Beraza, I., Adin, I., del Portillo, J., Sedano, B., Perez, N., Mendizábal, J.: EMC precertification laboratory for railway communication equipment. In: Technologies Applied to Electronics Teaching (TAEE), pp. 222–227 (2012)

10. Solas, G., Adin, I., Valdivia, Leonardo J., Arrizabalaga, S., Mendizabal, J.: Wireless communication emulator device and methodology for the ETCS BTM subsystem. In: Mendizabal, J., Berbineau, M., Vinel, A., Pfletschinger, S., Bonneville, H., Pirovano, A., Plass, S., Scopigno, R., Aniss, H. (eds.) Nets4Cars/Nets4Trains/Nets4Aircraft 2016. LNCS, vol. 9669, pp. 40–50. Springer, Cham (2016). doi:10.1007/978-3-319-38921-9_5

11. Heddebaut, M., Deniau, V., Rioult, J., Gransart, C.: Mitigation techniques to reduce the vulnerability of railway signaling to radiated intentional EMI emitted from a train. IEEE Trans. Electromagn. Compat. **PP**(99), 1–8 (2016)

12. González, R., Lubrani, P., de Miguel, G., Adín, I., Mendizabal, J.: EGNOS positioning in rail domain (ERSAT EAV). In: INC 2016. Royal institute of Navigation, Glasgow (2016)

13. Cross acceptance EMC test sites, test setup and test procedures specifications. Deliverable TREND project 30 April 2014

14. ERSAT EAV Grant Agreement No. 640747

Cyber Security for Railways – A Huge Challenge – Shift2Rail Perspective

Émilie Masson[1(✉)] and Christophe Gransart[2,3]

[1] Institut de Recherche Technologique Railenium, 59300 Famars, France
emilie.masson@railenium.eu
[2] University Lille Nord de France, 59000 Lille, France
[3] IFSTTAR, COSYS, 59650 Villeneuve d'Ascq, France
christophe.gransart@ifsttar.fr

Abstract. Currently, the wired and wireless networks used in the railway domain are usually heterogeneous, not enough protected and not fitted to the usual Cyber Security requirements in terms of sustainability, protection and attack detection. Some communication systems have already been protected by cryptographic techniques for instance. However, the quick evolution of the telecommunications means, the threats and the sustainability aspects have not been taken into account in this context. This paper aims at introducing the challenges of Railway sector to protect its infrastructure and to fulfil the requirements of Cyber Security.

1 Introduction

The development of Intelligent Transportation Systems (ITS) integrating Information and Communication Technologies (ICT) leads to the increase of services and features but also the increase of the surface of various kind of attacks. For instance, in the context of European Rail Traffic Management System (ERTMS), if a vulnerability is found, that vulnerability can impact all the systems across Europe. Railway systems are moving towards more intelligent and connected systems, which offers new opportunities of attackers and cyber-criminals. The security has to be considered in the transport domain for the protection of operators, for economic aspects and for the security of citizens. New goals appear with the increase of security, such as identification of assets and threats and identification of good Cyber Security practices.

The transport domain faces many challenges. First, there is no European law on Cyber Security for transport. Furthermore, the sector is still confronted with low level of awareness. Finally, Railway stakeholders have difficulties to dedicate budget for this specific topic (no contribution in terms of services and market share).

Cyber Security remains an increasingly important topic, especially for Railways. The Railway system represents a critical infrastructure. Each Railway and/or Infrastructure Manager has to protect its own infrastructure. The use of heterogeneous technologies and software solutions leads to very varied and disparate data sets.

The protection of these data implies a complex and multidimensional protection. The ever-increasing number of devices, processes and services implies an enormous amount of data to treat. The Cyber Security process has to be integrated at all phases of the

© Springer International Publishing AG 2017
A. Pirovano et al. (Eds.): Nets4Cars/Nets4Trains/Nets4Aircraft 2017, LNCS 10222, pp. 97–104, 2017.
DOI: 10.1007/978-3-319-56880-5_10

product lifecycle. The current trend is to make security-by-design, so that security is integrated into the development process since the beginning.

From an information security perspective, the main concern for Railway sector is to reduce the risk of potential data loss and ensure steady and stable rail operation. In case of problem, important consequences can appear, such as train stop (emergency braking, system failure), negative economic effects and loss of confidence and, in the worst case, the accident. Protection measures against cyber-attacks in the Railway sector are not yet fully developed. First, there is a lack of awareness of new risks. Second, the risks are not quite considered due to the high level of safety in the railway domain. The security aspects in the Railway sector are also strongly related to the safety of the system. The Cyber Security in the Railway domain consists in securing a safe system. The Cyber Security for Railways implies the protection of information systems against theft or damage, defence against attacks, external and internal risks...

The Fig. 1 illustrates a list of vulnerabilities and possible attacks of the Railway system. The different levels of attacks are highlighted, such as malwares at Operation Control Centre or interlocking, wireless attacks on wireless communications (GSM-R), password attack on Radio Block Centre, *etc.*

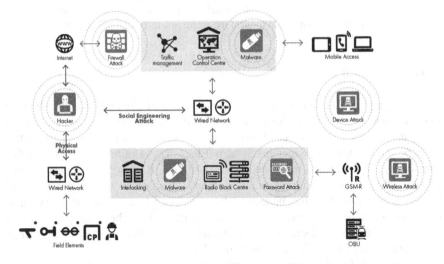

Fig. 1. Vulnerabilities and possible attacks on the Railway system from [1]

The paper presents an overview of the current situation of Railways regarding Cyber Security. Some examples of cyber-attacks are presented. The legal framework is highlighted and the current initiatives and projects are detailed. A focus on the works performed in the context of the Shift2Rail initiative is presented. Finally, we conclude.

2 Examples of Cyber-Attacks in the Railway Domain

Four specific examples of cyber-attacks on Railway system can be highlighted.

In 2008, a teenager derailed four tram trains in Lodz, Poland by using an adapted TV remote. Several injuries occurred.

In 2011 in the North Western of United State, pirates attacked remote computers, stopping the train signals for two days.

In 2015, North Korea was suspected of pirating subway system in Seoul for several months. Dozens of terminals were infested with malware.

Finally, in November 2016, the ticketing system of the BART at San Francisco was attacked by a ransomware that cyphers the hard disk of the ticket vending machines. During a weekend, the public transport infrastructure was available for free until a solution was found.

In all these examples, no incidents with dramatic consequences occurred but it demonstrated the vulnerability of the Railway systems.

3 Legal Framework

3.1 Set of Standards

For a systematic approach of information security, a set of standards was developed by industry associations and standardization bodies on security, such as:

- ISO 27001 (International Organization for Standardization), revision 2013: the most widespread worldwide, it covers aspects of information security management systems, mainly used by Railway operators;
- NIST SP800-53 (National Institute of Standards and Technology - US): it represents a more complete and current description than ISO 27001;
- ISA/IEC 62443 (International Society of Automation/International Electrotechnical Commission): it relies on a series of standards dealing with industrial communication networks – network and system security. It is mainly used by manufacturers;
- APTA (American Public Transportation Association): it consists in security and resource programs that help maintain and improve the security of resources, employees and customers;
- Network and Information Systems (NIS) Directive: it is a dedicated European regime corresponding to a directive on network and information system security. It is the main support tool for cyber-resilience in Europe with new requirements for network and information security for critical infrastructure operators;
- In France, EBIOS is a methodology pushed by the ANSSI (National Agency for Security of Information System). It must be used by the Vital Infrastructure Operators. That methodology is only used in France.

3.2 Zoom on NIST Framework

The NIST framework corresponds to the Framework for Improving Critical Infrastructure Cybersecurity. It represents a set of standards and best practices to help organizations managing Cyber Security risks in a cost-effective way. The standards is divided into 5 core functions presented in Table 1.

Table 1. Core functions of the NIST framework

Core function	Definition	Categories
Identify	An understanding of how to manage cybersecurity risks to systems, assets, data, and capabilities	Asset management, business environment, governance, risk assessment, risk management strategy
Protect	The controls and safeguards necessary to protect or deter cybersecurity threats	Access control, awareness and training, data security, data protection processes, maintenance, protective technologies
Detect	Continuous monitoring to provide proactive and real-time alerts of cybersecurity-related events	Anomalies and events, continuous monitoring, detection processes
Respond	Incident-response activities	Response planning, communications, analysis, mitigation, improvements
Recover	Business continuity plans to maintain resilience and recover capabilities after a cyber-breach	Recovery planning, improvements, communications

The other standards have more or less the same notions using sometime the same vocabulary but with different meanings. For instance, several methods are using the words like "threat", "consequence", "top event" but these words are similar but with different meanings for each standard. Mapping from one standard to another one is a difficult task. Moreover, each stakeholder has its own internal process to make security assessment so that sharing experience is difficult (when it is possible). Train manufacturers are also dependent of the requirements in terms of methodologies/standards required by their customers.

4   Research Projects Dedicated to Cyber Security for Railways

Previous and current projects already treated the topic of Cyber Security for Railways. This section is dedicated to the presentation of the main ones.

ERTMS/ETCS project
Some previous security studies were performed in the context of ERTMS/ETCS. The Cyber Security system should provide communication services also for signalling system and it is obvious that the security breaches can have serious safety consequences.

PROTECTRAIL project
PROTECTRAIL [2] objective was to integrate the growing influx of security technologies into rail operations and make them interoperable to improve security. For this

reason, PROTECTRAIL designed an interoperability framework built on a system-of-systems approach. This interoperability framework is a modular architectural framework into which asset-specific and interoperable security solutions can be "plugged", giving operators and infrastructure managers the possibility to continuously adapt their security systems to the changing security.

SECUR-ED project

The SECUR-ED [3] project was a demonstration project with an objective to provide a set of tools to improve urban transport security. Based on best practices, the SECUR-ED project integrated an interoperable mix of technologies and processes, covering different aspects; from risk assessment to complete training packages. These solutions also reflected the very diverse environment of mass transportation and also considered societal and legacy concerns.

CARONTE project

The aim of the CARONTE [4] project is to Create an Agenda for Research ON Transportation sEcurity. The objective of the project is then to define a future research agenda for security in land transport that focuses on core gaps caused by emerging risks while avoiding any doubling-up of research elsewhere.

SECRET project

The SECRET [5] project aims to assess the risks and consequences of intentional electromagnetic (EM) attacks on the rail infrastructure, to identify preventive and recovery measures and to develop protection solutions to ensure the security of the rail network, subject to intentional EM interferences, which can disturb many command-control, communication or signalling systems.

CIPSEC project

The objective of the CIPSEC project is to enhance Critical Infrastructure Protection with innovative SECurity framework. CIPSEC aims to develop a Security ecosystem through additional services including vulnerability testing, recommendations, training modules, standardization, protection against cascading effects, etc. The solutions and services will be evaluated in three environments: transport, health and environment.

5   Zoom on Shift2Rail Initiative

5.1   Introduction on the Joint Undertaking

Shift2Rail [6] is the first European rail joint technology initiative to seek focused research and innovation (R&I) and market-driven solutions by accelerating the integration of new and advanced technologies into innovative rail product solutions. Shift2Rail will promote the competitiveness of the European Rail Industry and will meet the changing EU transport needs. Through the R&I carried out within this Horizon2020 initiative, the necessary technology will be created to complete the Single European Railway Area (SERA).

The Joint Undertaking (JU) Shift2Rail is composed with 5 Innovation Programmes (IP) whose IP2 on Advanced Traffic Management and Control Systems.

The activities on IP2 started on September 2016, through the X2Rail-1 project, which involves 19 partners from the Railway sector coming from 9 countries (France, Germany, Belgium, Austria, Britain, Sweden, Spain, Italy, and the Czech Republic). The project covers various topics supported by 6 technical workpackages (WP).

5.2 Cyber Security in the Shift2Rail Context

One of the WPs of the X2Rail-1 project deal with Cyber Security for railways.

The main objectives of the WP dealing with Cyber Security are to define a Cyber Security system dedicated to railway and to define a security-by-design standard applicable to railway application.

The definition of a Cyber Security system consists in the specification of standardised interfaces, monitoring functions, protocol stacks and architectures for secure networks based, among others, on a security assessment of existing railway solutions and of railway networks. Efficiency and robustness of the standardised solution has to be demonstrated through a technical demonstrator. Security assessment, identification of the threat detection, prevention and response processes will be completed. A draft of the Cyber Security system specification will be provided at the end of the project.

The definition of a security-by-design standard applicable to railway application consists in specifying protection profiles and cyber security standards applicable to railway application and in demonstrating their applicability in a technical demonstrator. The definition of protection profiles and the identification of the cyber-secure development process will be completed. A draft of the security-by-design standard will be provided at the end of the project.

Railenium is involved in the Cyber Security activities of the Shift2Rail JU. Railenium aims at working on three specific topics.

The first one deals with the wireless part of the railway communication system: electromagnetic attacks on the system (declination of SECRET's work on LTE technologies, Wi-Fi), zoom on the detection part of attacks, development of a system based on SDR and protocol analysis.

The second topic will focus on the decision part. For a better identification of the attacks and performances, machine learning algorithms could also be used for the detection task. It would allow to: (1) Detect unknown (new) internal and external threats and intrusions, (2) Build models with incomplete knowledge about the normal behaviour, (3) Adapt the built models to changes used by the attackers to trick the security rules.

Finally, a last topic will work on human factors. The idea is to assess the professional human driver and central control station supervisor abilities to react to simulated cyber-attacks, or their consequences, in a realistic simulated environment.

5.3 Current Actions to Manage Cyber Security

In the project, we started a High-Level Security Assessment (HLSA) based on the IEC 62443 standard. We started to work on a common shared generic architecture which is representative of a real railway system based on ERTMS and using GSM-R communication system. According to the IEC 62443 standard, we defined the zones and conduits with their different security levels.

We are currently working on the Detailed Security Assessment which consists to list the assets, the threats, the impacts of the threats on the assets and the consequences on the system. For instance, on a Wi-Fi network for passengers we identified several threats concerning the jamming, deauthentication attacks to eject customers outside of the customer oriented network, fake access point to steal privacy information from passenger,… Some mitigation rules are proposed. A similar research has been done for GSM-R in the EU FP7 SECRET project (http://www.secret-project.eu/) [7]. We plan to conduct such a research for LTE based network too.

More generally, for all the kinds of threats, we are building a software framework, named Open Pluggable Framework (OPF), which is based on the concepts of autonomic systems. This framework (Fig. 2) monitors the environment using hardware and software probes. Then some algorithms detect abnormal behaviour using the data sent by the probes. Next, OPF decides how to react (with algorithms using machine learning methods) and finally applies several actions (e.g. an alarm or a reconfiguration).

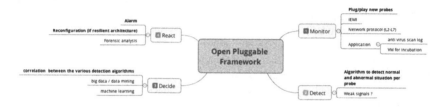

Fig. 2. The Open Pluggable Framework

Another action just started into the project concerns the security-by-design. In this action, the partners want to setup a set of rules concerning the development process of components with security properties. Finally, a reflection is carried out to create a Computer Emergency Response Team (CERT) dedicated to the railway environment, but currently we are just at the beginning of that process.

6   Conclusions and Perspectives

The objective of Cyber Security for railways is to move towards a Cyber Security standard for railways, equivalent to safety with EN 50126 [8], EN 50128 [9], EN 50129 [10], etc.

Safety is well managed by the railway industry through the lifecycle process of the development even if an upgrade of the system take several months to be certified. Once a train is certified, it can run for 30 years without any modification. The close link between "safety" and "security" has to be established. However, it is quite difficult to reconcile safety and security, which are antagonists on certain points. For instance, adding a security mechanism (ex. data encryption) can reach the safety because the system spends more time decoding messages and is therefore less reactive (with respect to real time). However, Cyber Security cannot follow the safety process based on certification. It will take too much time. For instance, a zero-day vulnerability must be solved as soon as possible. If not, the complete traffic of a country could be impacted or stopped. The impact on the economy/people of the country would be dramatic.

Several tools and practices have to be developed for securing the railway system, such as monitoring tool to detect, analyse and respond to threats and vulnerabilities, training of people, strongly linked to these monitoring tools, joint risk assessments, security-by-design, penetration testing, resilience, operation in degraded mode, information security policy, separation of critical and non-critical systems...

Acknowledgement. The authors would like to thank the European JU Shift2Rail and the French PIA who co-finances this research program.

References

1. Thales, Cybersecurity for Rail: Not A Single-Shot Approach, Applying the NIST approach to rail transportation, White Paper (2016)
2. PROTECTRAIL, Key Lessons for the Railway Sector on PROTECTRAIL Security Architecture, White Paper (2014)
3. SECUR-ED, SECured URban transportation – European Demonstration, White Paper (2014)
4. Bello, J.L., Viosca, E.G.: CARONTE project: Creating an Agenda for Research on Transportation Security. In: CIT2016 – XII Congreso de Ingeniería del Transporte, València, Universitat Politècnica de València (2016)
5. SECRET, security of railways against electromagnetic attacks, White Paper (2015)
6. Shift2Rail Joint Undertaking, Multi-Annual Action Plan. Technical report, November 2015
7. Heddebaut, M., Deniau, V., Rioult, J., Gransart, C.: Mitigation techniques to reduce the vulnerability of railway signaling to radiated intentional EMI Emitted From a Train. IEEE Trans. Electromagn. Compat. **PP**(99), 1–8 (2016)
8. EN 50126. Applications ferroviaires: spécification et démonstration de la fiabilité, de la disponibilité, de la maintenabilité et de la sécurité (FDMS). CENELEC, Comité Européen de Normalisation Électrotechnique (2000)
9. EN 50128. Railway applications — Communication, signalling and processing systems — Software for railway control and protection systems, EN50128 (2011)
10. EN 50129. Applications ferroviaires: systèmes de signalisation, de télécommunications et de traitement: systèmes électroniques de sécurité pour la signalisation. CENELEC, Comité Européen de Normalisation Électrotechnique (2003)

Nets4Cars

A Security Migration Concept for Vehicle-to-X Communication to Allow Long-Term PKI Operation

Jan-Felix Posielek$^{(\boxtimes)}$, Norbert Bißmeyer$^{(\boxtimes)}$, and Annika Strobel$^{(\boxtimes)}$

ESCRYPT GmbH, Lise-Meitner-Allee 4, 44801 Bochum, Germany
{jan-felix.posielek,norbert.bissmeyer,annika.strobel}@escrypt.com

Abstract. Applying appropriate security measures in wireless Vehicle-to-X (V2X) communication systems is very important since vehicles and roadside units must trust in information received over this channel. State-of-the-art V2X security solutions are based on Elliptic Curve Cryptography (ECC) using the NIST P-256 curve. For long-term use of such security infrastructure, updatability of security measures as well as cryptographic agility must be ensured.

In this paper a process for trust migration is proposed that maintains a fully functional Public Key Infrastructure (PKI) at all times for all entities. To ensure secure long-term operation, multiple security measures are highlighted, analyzed and evaluated. By adjusting the certificate format, new elliptic curves can be supported and flexibility is rendered possible. The evaluation provides a comprehensive analysis and identifies the steps required to deploy a secure and reliable V2X PKI even if cryptographic algorithms change in the future.

1 State-of-the-Art Vehicle-to-X Security

The digitalization of transportation systems, especially the automotive industry, provides many benefits. If vehicles and infrastructure are able to communicate with each other, new innovative possibilities arise that increase safety and efficiency. Also the collection and analysis of usage data may provide additional benefits. All these advanced applications of technology in transportation are collected in an Intelligent Transport System (ITS) whose roll-out is strategically planned in the European Union (EU) [4].

The current specification for certificate formats and security header in a European V2X PKI is based on the European Telecommunications Standards Institute (ETSI) Technical Specification (TS) 103 097 in version 1.2.1 [7]. The asymmetric cryptographic algorithms rely on ECC which combines the advantages of asymmetric cryptography and small keys. The specification makes use of the National Institute of Standards and Technology (NIST) P-256 elliptic curve exclusively and does not specify any other curves. This may lead to problems for the long-term operation of the PKI if algorithms or specific curves are attacked or weaken over time.

© Springer International Publishing AG 2017
A. Pirovano et al. (Eds.): Nets4Cars/Nets4Trains/Nets4Aircraft 2017, LNCS 10222, pp. 107–118, 2017.
DOI: 10.1007/978-3-319-56880-5_11

Also, currently, there is no process defined for updating the trust anchor's key. Cryptographic keys should always be bound to validity restrictions that prohibit an infinite use. A trade off has to be found when choosing this duration. Whereas a short period makes it hard for attackers, the roll-out of a new key must be organized with the affected entities. When the lifetime is long, attackers have more time and may put the system at risk when the key is exposed.

Therefore a migration process is developed to allow updating of Certificate Authority (CA) certificates. In this context, the migration of cryptographic algorithms is tested to allow long-term PKI operation. The goal is to enable switching the underlying elliptic curve during operation while preserving functionality for all entities. In this paper, we evaluate the requirements, necessary steps, options and consequences with the example of a migration from the NIST P-256 curve [13] to the Brainpool-P256R1 and Brainpool-P384R1 curve [12].

2   Related Work

To analyze the requirements for long-term operation of a V2X PKI as specified by the ETSI [5] and implemented by the Car-to-Car (C2C) Communication Consortium (C2C-CC) [2], related work in the fields of long-term use of cryptography and trust migration is considered.

2.1   Long-Term Use of Cryptography

Cryptographic keys provide the basis for most security solutions. For long-term use, there are two main aspects that must be considered. First, the key length must be sufficiently large. Second, the validity of a cryptographic key must be limited. As for the current standing of research, post-quantum cryptography relies on large keys which renders these algorithms inapplicable for V2X [11].

Elliptic curve cryptography, which belongs to the public key schemes, is very attractive since keys with a length of 250 bits suffice to achieve a security level comparable to 128 bits in symmetric cryptography. Therefore elliptic curves are the preferred choice for an ITS. As of 2016, TOP SECRET purposes require NIST P-384, so an elliptic curve with a key length of 384 bit [14].

It is important to specify a limited lifetime for keys because any key can be cracked with brute-force methods and sufficient computation power and time. Also, through carelessness, espionage, or advancements in cryptanalysis, the probability that a key is compromised over time increases constantly. With research advancing on attacks on cryptographic algorithms, it is important to update keys regularly to sustain flexibility — a process which is known as key rollover [10].

The security operational considerations for Domain Name System (DNS) states that unless there are extraordinary circumstances, the lifetime of long term keys should not significantly exceed a period of four years. A rollover should be conducted at least every year [10]. The choice of the validity period is always a trade off between adequate security and resource consumption since too short validities always come with the overhead of the rollover process.

2.2 Trust Migration

The migration of security components must be well defined in order to be carried out smoothly and to assure continous operation. If done infrequently, the risk that operational problems occur increases.

The Bundesamt für Sicherheit in der Informationstechnik (BSI) proposes a CA certificate rollover plan for Smart Meter [3]. Here, there are also three layers: Root Certificate Authority (RCA), sub-CA, and end entity. The lower layers implement an overlap time when a new certificate is retrieved. The RCA implements an additional feature: besides a new self-signed root certificate, a link certificate is issued. The link certificate includes the same public keys as the new root certificate but instead of being self-signed, it is signed by the old root certificate. All entities in the PKI use it to transfer the trust from the old root certificate to the new root certificate.

Another migration concept is used in DNS Security Extensions (DNSSEC) which is used to provide authenticity for DNS data provided to users on the Internet. As the signing key for DNS records has a limited lifetime, a rollover process is defined that comes with certain challenges with respect to cached information as pointed out by Kolkman et al. [10]. There are two ways to accomplish smooth operation: key pre-publication and double signatures.

Key Pre-publication. When a new key is generated, it is not used for signing operations at first but only distributed to all entities. After the pre-publication, all signatures are generated with the new key and the old key is removed.

Double Signatures. All data is signed with the old key and with the new key as well during a specified overlap time. This ensures that all entities can verify data signed with either key. After the overlap time, the old key and all signatures with the old key are removed.

3   Trust Migration for V2X Security

Since certificates in PKIs have a limited validity period, CAs must update their certificates periodically. In this section, we introduce a trust migration process that defines how this process is performed for a V2X PKI according to ETSI TS 102 940 [5] which ensures that the system is fully functional the entire time.

To do so, we employ the concept of link certificates for our trust migration process in V2X similar to the Smart Meter PKI proposed by the BSI [3]. However, since V2X communication must keep the security overhead as small as possible, attaching the entire certificate chain to a message is not feasible. Also, double signatures lead to a vast overhead. To solve this, we use the concept of pre-publication similar to the implementation in DNSSEC.

The definition of a process is mainly required for safety reasons. By using a link certificate, a manual trust transfer or a proprietary solution is rendered obsolete. The pre-loading ensures that the PKI is not irregularly stressed during transition. Also, all cars can verify received messages at all times so that no information is dismissed.

3.1   Migration of the Root Certificate

The migration of the root certificate is the most difficult since it is the trust anchor. Certificates on lower layers can be switched more easily since the trust is provided by the signature of the root certificate. We make use of a so called link certificate. Whereas a root certificate is always self-signed using the key of the certificate itself, a link certificate contains the keys of the new certificate but is signed using the key of the old certificate. It is a useful tool for exchanging a root certificates but it is not permitted for non-self-signed certificates since that would remove control from the RCA. The link certificate also shall not be used to sign any other certificates but only to transfer the trust.

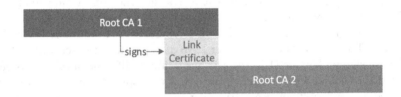

Fig. 1. The trust of the expiring root certificate is transfered using a link certificate.

In Fig. 1, the trust transfer using the link certificate is depicted. A new root certificate must be generated before the old root certificate, here labeled as Root CA 1, expires in order to ensure continuous operation. When generating the new root certificate, here called Root CA 2, a link certificate containing the keys of the new root certificate is issued with a signature of the old certificate. The link certificate must not exceed the validity of the old RCA. Therefore, during the overlap time, all entities must receive the new root certificate in combination with the link certificate in order to perform the trust transfer before the old certificate becomes invalid.

3.2   Transition Timing

In order to provide continuous operation, it is specified how the transition is performed so that a new root certificate is distributed to all entities. Stations receive the initial root certificate during production as trust anchor. Sub-CA certificates, e.g., for the Authorization Authority (AA) which issues the Authorization Tickets (ATs) used for ITS-G5 communication by the vehicles, are retrieved on demand during operation [6].

The transition is split into two phases as illustrated in Fig. 2. When a new certificate is generated along with its link certificate, the preloading phase starts. At this time, the old certificate is still exclusively used for issuing certificates. The new certificate must not be used to issue any certificates that have a validity that starts before the seconds phase. This period is shown grayed out for Authorization Authority 2. Otherwise entities may receive messages with a certificate

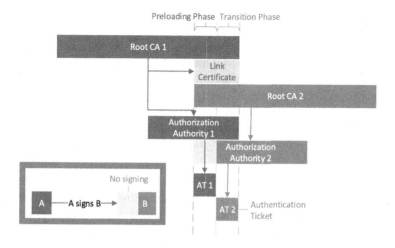

Fig. 2. Certificate issuance during transition.

chain to the new root certificate that they do not trust yet. The duration of the preloading period must be chosen in accordance with the maintenance times of the end entities in the ITS domain so that all stations get the chance to retrieve the new trust anchor. We assume that some stations do not have ubiquitous Internet access and need maintenance to get certificate updates.

The second phase, the transition phase, starts when the CA applies the new keys for message signing and certificate issuance operations. From then on, the new certificate is used for issuance operations exclusively since all entities shall have received the new root certificate at this point in time. Since the distribution of certificates signed with the new root does not take place for all sub-CAs and ITS stations at once, the second part of the overlap time also requires a certain time. Therefore, the old root certificate is still valid but only used for verification purposes of received messages.

At the end of the transition phase, the old root certificate expires and the PKI returns to regular operation. The link certificate loses validity as well, as it is only used to transfer the trust of the old to the new certificate. It is never used for any signing operations.

4   Security Migration Measures

The security formats for certificates and messages in V2X communication are specified in ETSI TS 103 097 [7]. A main requirement of Intelligent Transport Systems is a small message size, since the channel capacity is very limited. Therefore the overhead for security shall be as small as possible. As of version 1.2.1 of this standard, the entire system is based on the NIST P-256 elliptic curve as specified in FIPS 186 by the NIST [13]. For long-term operation, using other curves with potentially larger key size must be considered.

4.1 Adding New Elliptic Curves

All entities in the ITS domain must support a newly added curve, which poses the main challenge. If only a limited number of stations would switch the curve, old systems are not able to verify messages signed using the new curve. There are options to weaken this requirements: if the ATs used by end entities keep using the same curve and only CA certificates are migrated, the trust anchor is cryptographically strengthened while the performance requirements for ITS-G5 communication are not obstructed. In the following, two different migration scenarios are discussed.

Migration of All Certificates. The CAs according to ETSI TS 102 940 [5] each hold a certificate to authenticate their public keys. ITS stations are in possession of several certificates: an Enrollment Credential (EC) and multiple Authorization Tickets (ATs). When migrating every certificate to a new curve, every entity must be able to generate signatures, verify them and possibly perform encryption and decryption. With that comes also the performance requirement. Especially messages signed with an AT must be processed quickly, which is commonly achieved using special cryptographic acceleration for each curve implemented in the automotive Hardware Security Module (HSM). Thus, every HSM must support and should be optimized for the new curve.

Migration of CA Certificates. As already discussed, the signature generation and verification of messages using an AT is most critical. The verification of CA certificates is not as time-critical and must often only be performed once. This leads to the option to only migrate CA certificates to a new curve. The ITS-G5 communication is still secured with AT keys using the old unbroken and valid curve as well as the EC for management purposes. The verification of CA certificates using the new curve can be done in software without hardware-accelerated cryptography.

Since ATs shall have a short validity period by definition, the use of a curve with short keys does not pose as big of threat as the use of such curve for certificates with long validity when it comes to long-term PKI operation. Therefore, the option to only update CA certificates is a desirable option for long-term operation without penalizing old hardware.

4.2 Security Header and Certificate Formats

To allow long-term operation of a V2X PKI by adding the new elliptic curves, the currently specified security header and certificate formats in ETSI TS 103 097 version 1.2.1 must be adjusted [7]. The adjustments can be made in different ways, which is discussed to identify a simple yet long lasting solution.

Extending the Public Key Algorithm Enumeration. An obvious solution is to extend the enumeration of public key algorithms. Currently one byte combines multiple parameters separated by an underscore: the algorithm, such as Elliptic Curve Digital Signature Algorithm (ECDSA), the elliptic curve, e.g., NIST P-256, and, if applicable, the hash function, e.g., SHA256.

The enumeration can be extended with new values for the curve, e.g., Brainpool-P256R1, Brainpool-P384R1, or NIST P-384, with the Secure Hash Algorithm (SHA) hash function corresponding to the field size.

Listing 1.1. Proposal for a modified `CryptoParameters` enumeration.

```
enum {
    ecdsa_nistp256_with_sha256 (0),
    ecies_nistp256 (1),
    reserved (240..253),
    useParentCurve (254)
    useDomainParameters (255),
    (2^8 − 1)
} CryptoParameters;
```

Listing 1.2. Proposal for a modified `PublicKeyAlgorithm` struct.

```
struct {
    CryptoParameters curve;
    select (curve) {
    case useDomainParameters:
        opaque      p<var>;
        opaque      a<var>;
        opaque      b<var>;
        opaque      seed<var>;
        EccPoint base;
        opaque      order<var>;
        uint8      cofactor;
    }
} PublicKeyAlgorithm;
```

Flexible Curve Specification. Currently, the `PublicKeyAlgorithm` enumeration makes adding a new elliptic curve difficult since it must be added to the ETSI standard first. We propose to add the possibility to specify a curve with its domain parameters in addition to parameter inheritance.

Listing 1.1 shows the definition of the `CryptoParameters` enumeration. We provide two new ways to specify the employed elliptic curve. If `useParentCurve` is used, the curve parameters of the issuing certificate are used. This can be done recursively until a CA certificate containing the parameters is reached. Additionally, the curve itself can be specified by its describing values and the `useDomainParameters` value.

The `PublicKeyAlgorithm` field is changed from an enumeration to a struct as shown in Listing 1.2. The struct combines the enumerated value with the optional fields for the domain parameters. If the curve is a regular enumerated item, no additional data is appended. This is also the case if the parent curve shall be used. The `useDomainParameters` value leads to the inclusion of all data required to specify the entire curve.

Since every certificate contains at least two public key specifications, one for the verification key and one for the signature, using the inheritance for the signature is favorable since it is always dependent on the signing key.

Consequences. Both options require an update for all entities of the V2X PKI. The adjustments differ in two ways: First, the size of the certificate may increase. Second, the performance when parsing may be different, albeit only marginally.

While the extension of the enumeration alone may be easier to implement, for every addition of an elliptic curve the specification must be updated. The introduction of custom domain parameters provides more flexibility.

5   Evaluation

In this chapter, the security migration for different scenarios is tested in practice and evaluated with the focus on the communication between ITS stations. We use a real-world implementation of a V2X PKI and simulate the communication of an ITS station using a Java client.

Table 1. Parameters for certificate generation used in our analysis.

Field	Root	EA	AA	EC	AT
Name	RXX	EXX	AXX	Module ID	
Verification key	✓	✓	✓	✓	✓
Encryption key	✓	✓	✓	✗	✗
Assurance level	0x80	0x80	0x80	0x80	0x80
Region	None	None	None	None	None
AID/SSP		36, 37	36, 37	36/0x00, 37/0x00	36/0x00, 37/0x00
Signer	Self	RXX	RXX	EXX	AXX

In order to obtain comparable results, the parameters for ITS certificates are defined in Table 1. All flexible parameters in our analysis are chosen according to the use case. The validity times are current timestamps with a period of 1 day in between start and end time. Besides the certificates, the impact on a `SecuredMessage` is analyzed that is used for Cooperative Awareness Message (CAM) [9] among others. In our analysis, we generate a `SecuredMessage` for the ITS-AID 36 with the signer info set to `certificate_digest_with_sha256` and an empty payload.

The following objective information is collected by an end entity during the migration:

Size. The most critical metric is the certificate size, especially for Authorization Tickets. The size of each certificate, the security header of a Secured Message (SM), and security management messages is evaluated.

Performance. The signature verification is performed for the certificate itself and not the entire chain. Our measurements are performed on a machine with an Intel Core i5-6500 CPU at 3.20 GHz using the Bouncy Castle implementation [15] in a Java client software that simulates the ITS stations. To obtain reproducible results, every signature is verified 1000 times. Since this metric is extremely dependent on the implementation, especially for the cryptographic operation, the results are put in relation with manufacturer's product specification such as verification speeds of a HSM for specific elliptic curves.

Storage. The amount of storage required for the certificate and private keys for end entities is be analyzed as well. We differentiate between secured storage and unsecured storage. All private keys are stored securely. All certificates, with the exception of the root certificate, may be stored in unsecured storage.

There are criteria that have to be taken into account that cannot be measured but have an impact on the migration. We discuss each metric individually for each use case.

Implementation. Since the migration of the PKI must be performed by all entities, every manufacturer has to support the changes. Therefore the implementation effort has to be weighted to make a statement on the feasibility.

Hardware. The hardware may be required to be updated if new elliptic curves must be supported. When adding new elliptic curves, the verification performance needs have to be met for certain use cases such as the verification of secured messages with the corresponding AT.

Flexibility. The employed certificate formats differ in their flexibility when looking at long-term usage. If new curves can be added easily without updates of the specification, the system can be maintained easily over longer periods of time.

Key Length. Without looking at the flexibility of the format, the key length of the elliptic curve plays an important role for long term deployment.

Each use case is evaluated for every metric. In order to provide a comprehensive yet easy overview, a rating scale is introduced.

⊕ The plus symbol indicates a good solution and that the changes of this use case provide benefits, e.g., with respect to the aim of achieving cryptographic agility within the boundaries of that metric.

○ The empty circle shows that only a negligible advantage or disadvantage, if any, is given through the use case-specific changes for this metric.

⊖ A minus is used to rate if the adjustments add limitations to the system and careful considerations have to be applied.

5.1   Use Cases

We evaluate the migration scenarios for a V2X PKI based on the comparison of the implementation using ETSI TS 103 097 in version 1.2.1 [7] and the adjustments recommended in Sect. 4. To evaluate the consequences, the conducted Use Cases (UCs) are defined and listed in Table 2.

Table 2. Overview of evaluated use case.

Use case	Elliptic curve	Impact	Format
UC0	NIST P-256	All entities	Reference implementation
UC1	Brainpool-P256R1	All entities	Flexible format, enumeration
UC2	Brainpool-P384R1	RCA	Flexible format, domain parameters
	Brainpool-P256R1	EA, AA, EC, AT	Flexible format, enumeration

The reference implementation [7] is analyzed in UC0. The effects of using a different curve while applying the proposed flexible format with enumerated items, as introduced in Sect. 4.2, are evaluated in UC1. Here, it is migrated to the Brainpool-P256R1 curve. UC2 depicts the effects of using a larger curve using domain parameters in the flexible format for the trust anchor.

Table 3. Subjective evaluation of the reference implementation.

Type	Certificate or message [byte]			Verification [ms]		
	UC0	UC1	UC2	UC0	UC1	UC2
RCA	224	224	908	7	8	20
EA	236	236	268	7	8	20
AA	236	236	268	7	8	20
EC	184	184	184	7	8	8
AT	168	168	168	7	8	8
SM	93	93	93	7	8	8

5.2 Results

The objective results are presented for all use cases in Table 3. The size of a certificate is dependent on the information it includes. Since the RCA, Enrollment Authority (EA), and AA also include an encryption key, the certificates are respectively larger. The AT which does not include any identifying information is the smallest certificate type. A SM with the signer provided as certificate digest is only 93 byte. The verification time in software for signatures using NIST P-256, as applied in UC0, is the same for all types with 7 ms.

UC1 shows that the size remains unchanged for the proposed format adjustments when the enumeration is used. When it comes to performance, our measurements showed that signature verifications with the Brainpool curve take 1 ms longer which is in accordance to the specifications of HSM manufacturers [1]. The storage requirements remain unchanged. Many HSMs support the Brainpool-P256R1 curve out-of-the-box so that for most entities, no hardware changes are required. No additional security is gained since the key length remains the same but the format provides the flexibility to easily adapt the curve without touching the standard.

Table 4. Cumulative evaluation of all use case.

Use Case	Size	Performance	Storage	Implementation	Hardware	Flexibility	Key Length
UC0	⊕	⊕	⊕	⊕	⊕	⊖	⊖
UC1	⊕	⊕	⊕	○	⊕	⊕	⊖
UC2	⊕	⊕	○	○	⊕	⊕	⊕

An effective solution is to employ domain parameters for the RCA whereas all other entities use the flexible format with the enumeration with no overhead. For ITS-G5 communication, curves with more than 256 bit are currently not feasible due to the increased computational overhead for signature verifications. Here, the overhead is more than twice as much with 20 ms per verification for Brainpool-P384R1. Therefore EA, AA, EC, AT and consequential SM use the Brainpool-P256R1 curve for their keys. The trust anchor can be properly secured with a larger key length. The signatures for the sub-CA certificates slightly increase in size but by using the referral to the issuing certificate for the algorithmic parameters, the overhead is maintainable.

In Table 4, an overview of the considered use cases is shown with the respective impact rated according to our defined scale. Considering the objective of long-term operation, some evaluated metrics can be given a lower priority. The implementation effort for the flexible format may come at a high cost in the beginning but pays off on the long run as it is only required once. Also the storage requirements are negligible since the overhead that comes with larger keys does not exceed the storage possibilities of modern HSMs [1]. Elliptic curves with a key length of 256 bit can be highly optimized and accomplish the performance requirements [8] for ITS-G5 communication.

The most important metrics for long-term operation are flexibility and key length. Flexibility can only be accomplished by employing the proposed format changes. By using elliptic curves with key lengths of at least 384 bits for the RCA, long-term operation is secured.

6   Conclusion

The security migration of a V2X PKI as specified by ETSI is evaluated with this paper. Based on existing solutions to long-term deployment, a process for trust migration that performs the rollover of the root certificate while preserving full functionality for all entities at all times is proposed. The specific circumstances of a V2X PKI are taken into account to provide a process where every entity can retrieve the new root certificate before it receives messages that are signed under the new root certificate. This avoids that messages cannot be verified and potential safety-related actions cannot be performed due to security reasons.

Two groups of security measures are highlighted: elliptic curves and the security formats. As there is only a single elliptic curve currently employed in V2X communication the use of alternative curves for long-term deployment is vital. In order to do so, the current security format is evaluated and adjustments are proposed to make it more flexible. The impact is evaluated for different metrics based on multiple use cases. By employing the format adjustments that we proposed, flexibility is achieved that allows to use new elliptic curves, even potentially unknown curves, while keeping the certificate and message size for the end entities small. Using different elliptic curves for ITS-G5 communication and the trust anchor on top of the hierarchy leads to a solution that is high-performance for deployment nowadays while being secure for long-term deployment.

For large-scale deployment, the use of a trust list is under discussion where a trusted operator provides a cryptographically signed list of trusted RCAs. Essentially, it introduces another layer on top of the RCA. The proposed trust migration process requires to be adjusted for this architectural change.

References

1. Autotalks: Autotalks V2X Security Portfolio. Technical report, Autotalks, September 2014. http://www.auto-talks.com/wp-content/uploads/2014/09/Autotalks_White_Paper_V2X_Security_Portfolio_V1.3_COMPANY.pdf
2. Bißmeyer, N., Stübing, H., Schoch, E., Götz, S., Stotz, J.P., Lonc, B.: A generic public key infrastructure for securing car-to-X communication. In: 18th ITS World Congress, Orlando, vol. 14 (2011)
3. BSI: Smart Metering PKI - Public Key Infrastruktur für Smart Meter Gateways. TR 03109-4, BSI, v1.1.1, May 2015
4. European Commission: A European Strategy on Cooperative Intelligent Transport Systems, a Milestone Towards Cooperative, Connected and Automated Mobility, November 2016
5. ETSI: Intelligent Transport Systems (ITS); Security; ITS Communications Security Architecture and Security Management. TS 102 940, ETSI, v1.1.1, June 2012
6. ETSI: Intelligent Transport Systems (ITS); Security; Trust and Privacy Management. TS 102 941, ETSI, v1.1.1, June 2012
7. ETSI: Intelligent Transport Systems (ITS); Security; Security Header and Certificate Formats. TS 103 097, ETSI, v1.2.1, June 2013
8. ETSI: Intelligent Transport Systems (ITS); V2X Applications; Part 3: Longitudinal Collision Risk Warning (LCRW) Application Requirements Specification. TS 101 539-3, ETSI, v1.1.1, November 2013
9. ETSI: Intelligent Transport Systems (ITS); Vehicular Communications; Basic Set of Applications; Part 2: Specification of Cooperative Awareness Basic Service. EN 302 637-2, ETSI, v1.3.2, November 2014
10. Kolkman, O., Gieben, R.: DNSSEC Operational Practices. RFC 4641 (Informational). http://www.ietf.org/rfc/rfc4641.txt. Obsoleted by RFC 6781
11. Lange, T.: Initial recommendations of long-term secure post-quantum systems. In: PQCrypto (2015)
12. Lochter, M., Merkle, J.: Elliptic Curve Cryptography (ECC) Brainpool Standard Curves and Curve Generation (2010)
13. NIST: Digital Signature Standard (DSS). FIPS 186-4, NIST, August 2013
14. NSA: Commercial National Security Algorithm (CSNA) Suite. Technical report, NSA, January 2016
15. The Legion of the Bouncy Castle: Bouncy Castle Crypto API (2016)

Multi-sensor Tracking System: Towards More Intelligent Roads

Olatz Iparraguirre Gil[1(✉)], Borja Nuñez Barrionuevo[1], Joshua Puerta Prieto[1],
Luis Matey Muñoz[1], Irantzu Bores[2], and Alfonso Brazalez Guerra[1(✉)]

[1] Ceit-IK4, Pº Mikeletegi, 48, 20009 Donostia - San Sebastián, Spain
{oiparraguirre,bnbarrionuevo,jpuerta,lmatey,abrazalez}@ceit.es
[2] Gertek, Alameda Gregorio de la Revilla, 27, 48010 Bilbao, Spain
i.bores@gerteksa.com

Abstract. Road Safety is a major societal issue, and the EU Commission has adopted an ambitious programme, which sets out a mix of initiatives focussing on the improvement of vehicle and infrastructure safety and road user behaviour. The road conditions play a very important role in this target up to the extent that it is an indispensable information for infrastructure managers who alert road users about driving conditions. Nowadays, some static cameras installed on the main highway stretches detect events like fallen trees, obstacles on the road or traffic jams. In addition, meteorological condition information is given by weather stations. However, these resources have some limitations, they cannot cover the whole road network infrastructure and the information they provide is not very precise. A solution for this matter lies in the use of fleets as a multi-sensor tracking system in order to give a better service of real time traffic information. The purpose of this paper is to describe how this solution could be addressed in the framework of a project under development by Ceit and Gertek.

Keywords: Road safety · Road condition · Alert · Driving condition · Multi-sensor tracking system · Real time traffic information

1 Introduction

Weather conditions have a strong influence on the traffic flows and its impact on safety is remarkable: in Spain approximately 17% of the annual vehicle crashes are weather-related [1].

Meteorological conditions are directly related with driving conditions. Snow and rain, as well as fog, reduce the visibility, but also vehicle performance, increasing the risk of having an accident due to slippery roads and wind speed alters the stability of the vehicle. The presence of adverse weather conditions normally implies traffic flow contraction, speed reduction and increase in density [2]. Thus, driving behaviour should be adapted to the environment in order to decrease the risk of crashes. For this aim, weather information systems are needed to warn road users about the driving conditions.

Alerting drivers about road situation is responsibility of infrastructure managers. However, traffic management in real time is a complex task since it means to control a

© Springer International Publishing AG 2017
A. Pirovano et al. (Eds.): Nets4Cars/Nets4Trains/Nets4Aircraft 2017, LNCS 10222, pp. 119–127, 2017.
DOI: 10.1007/978-3-319-56880-5_12

huge and distributed extension. Nowadays, the traffic management systems that support this activity are static cameras, meteorological stations and information systems such as Variable Message Signs (VMS), Radio Data System-Traffic Message Channel (RDS-TMC) etc. Nevertheless, those resources present some important disadvantages: they require to be constantly monitored by road operators and, what is more, these resources cannot cover the complete road network.

Events that are bound to cause traffic difficulties such as fallen trees, obstacles, jams, accidents etc. are supervised through road cameras in the control centre. The road operators analyse the images and warn drivers about which conditions they will find in the roadway. Unfortunately, there are still many kilometres to cover in the main roads and practically all of the less frequented roads.

The detection of weather-related events is supported by meteorological stations, which are fixed at a point and quite distant one from another, leading to low accuracy measurement. This system is not able to identify very located events like ice sheets. So in adverse weather situations the warning is shown for a wide road stretch and with greatly generic advices.

Considering the mentioned issues, TrafikData project is a potential solution since it develops a real-time log of roadway conditions and it is independent from the infrastructure. TrafikData uses probe vehicles in road-maintenance fleets equipped with on-board electronics that allow the use of vehicles as sensors.

The purpose of this paper is to explain how this solution is being addressed, present the final objectives of the project, describe the general architecture of the system and emphasize on the fog detection system.

2   Objectives

The development of this project pretends to:

- Reinforce the improvement of the current traffic management systems.
- Develop a value added robust solution that integrates advanced technologies in a flexible way and with a reasonable cost.
- To boost the environmental sustainability through the road security increase.

   Within these general objectives, the main targets of TrafikData project are:

- To obtain a system capable of identifying in real time potentially dangerous events concerning road security.
- To obtain an automatic system capable of generating meteorological maps in real time.
- To obtain an automatic system that generates signalling maps which makes easier the road maintenance and error identifications.

   Looking from a functional point of view it is also important to ensure that the product is scalable so as it enables to add more services in the future associated with the use of vehicle as data sources.

3 System Description

Looking forward to the improvement of road safety and intending to provide infrastructure managers a reliable monitoring system, the target of this project is to develop a multi-sensor on board platform. This multi-sensor tracking system is compound by two main sections: On Board Unit and Back Office, which are defined below.

3.1 On Board Unit (OBU)

The OBU in this phase of the project consists on the integration of different sensors, which gather useful information for monitoring road conditions.

Camera. The probe vehicle has a dash camera for fog detection. It is continuously taking snapshots of the road and analysing the images at the same time. The image processing works out the percentage of pixels that are under the established greyscale limit. This percentage is used for calculating the visibility of the road.

Meteor. Meteor is a device developed by Gertek for premature detection of ice sheets. It is designed to be attached to the door of a vehicle thanks to some magnets and it has three sensors to measure ground and air temperature and humidity. With these parameters, Meteor can predict icy roads.

Rain Sensor. Rain sensor is a switching device for the detection of rainfall. Placed in the windshield, this device senses rain by attending the principle of total internal reflection. The output of this sensor enables to differentiate between three levels: no rain, light rain and heavy rain.

OBD. An OBD device is installed to gather all the information the vehicle provides (e.g. rpm, speed, ambient air temperature, barometric pressure etc.). In that way, it enables the study of traffic flow in relation with road conditions or the verification of some already measured data such as ambient temperature.

GPS. The location data in real time allows matching each measurement with a GIS position, which is essential for the objective of the project. In this way, road managers know meteorological and traffic information of every specific location of the infrastructure.

3.2 Back Office

The Back Office is the control and management centre of TrafikData system, it has a modular design and handles all the collected information. The application allows to display and process the information for meteorological, ambient or traffic management purposes.

4   Architecture

4.1   Software Architecture

TrafikData was designed for been a scalable embedded device, and therefore it presents a modular software architecture (Fig. 1). It is composed by OBD, Rain, Fog and Meteor modules that gather information from the road, the main module which is the Control Unit of the system, and the web server that makes the data fusion and displays the information through the Smartphone.

The control and configuration of TrafikData system is managed by the main module. This module uses a machine-to-machine (M2 M) protocol to intercommunicate through internet with an external server. It handles the writing and reading of the Data Base, the configuration of the modules, the communication with the back office and the smartphone, the stop and start up of processes and the register and synchronization of the GPS receptor.

The software architecture is based on a Servlet Container, which integrates all the different modules.

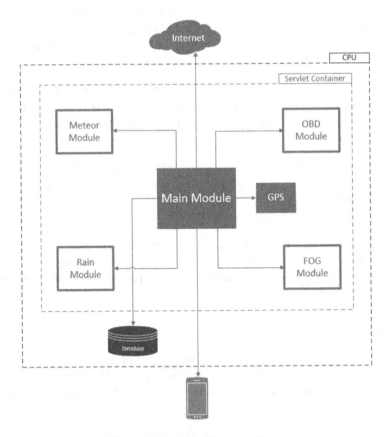

Fig. 1. Software architecture schema

This Software is installed on a Windows on-board computer. The Windows Service Control Manager is responsible for launching automatically all the services needed by the system for working. Firstly, every module of the system is synchronized with the time and date of the GPS, next, these are configured from Back Office and finally the main module is launched for running indefinitely until the user stops the system.

4.2 Hardware Architecture

The hardware architecture, as well as the software architecture, is modular. The main module is executed on the embedded computer where the rest of the hardware is connected to (Fig. 2).

Fog module is composed of a HD web cam, OBD module consist of an OBD-II advanced Wi-fi device, Meteor is a Bluetooth embedded solution designed by Gertek and Rain module incorporate an analog rain and light sensor. TrafikData system also integrates an USB GPS receptor and a car-wifi router that makes the communication system operative. The Smartphone is the tool for the driver to monitor the data in real-time, which is very useful especially in the validation phase of the project.

For the aim of building a portable and wireless device, TrafikData system is provided with three different power supplies: an external battery to supply the CPU and the rain sensor controller and a car plug output to connect the router.

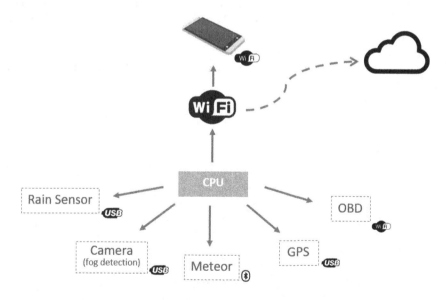

Fig. 2. Hardware architecture schema

5   Fog Detection

So far, most of the work that has been focused on detecting and rating different types of weather conditions has typically involved the use of special sensors such as radars, visibilitymeters or disdrometers. However, due to the high cost of these components, standard cameras are considered a viable alternative.

The different adverse climatic conditions vary depending on the size of the particles that compose those conditions. In this way, we can classify them as static or dynamic elements.

Fog or mist, are concerned with static environmental conditions due to the fact that they are small particles, and therefore, usually spatially and temporally consistent. In consequence, the effect does not vary significantly in time and space so it can be analysed in a more individual way. [3] for example aims to interpret one or several scenes with misty weather and study the appearance to identify fog and mist through the colours. On the other hand [4], it is able to automatically detect the fog and estimate visibility distances through a dynamic implementation of Koschmieder's law.

Finally, a method that integrates three different filters has been used consisting of an analysis of the HSV characteristics and the image grayscale [5].

6   Validation

Currently, the project is in its validation phase. The system has been mounted in a prove car to test different routes. Some itineraries have been fixed taking into account different road geometries such as highways, local roads, mountain trails etc. It is also concerned to do tests depending on the weather conditions to try and calibrate meteorological sensors.

The results of a significant test are shown below (Fig. 3). This try-out was done in a cloudy day with some periods of light rain, the track includes a first stage inside the city road and a second stage on a mountain road.

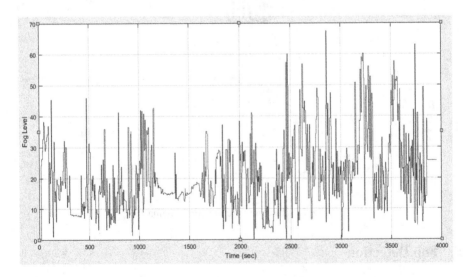

Fig. 3. Original fog level in time scale

Figure 3 shows the original fog level signal. The noise that appears might be related with a high density of curves and road slopes, which causes an abrupt change of greyscale values. To filter this oscillations, the mean of the last minute values is done for each analysed point. In addition, the vehicle speed is used to display the fog level in relation with distance, which gives a perspective of the size of the fog bank.

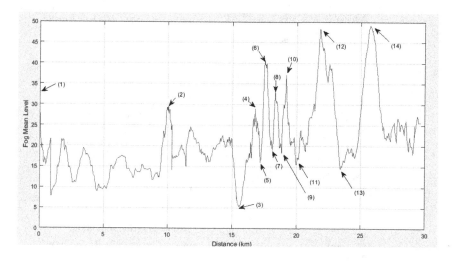

Fig. 4. Fog mean level analysis in relation with distance

As it is shown above (Fig. 4), the first half of the route went on under 25% of fog level which is considered as no-fog, whereas, in the second part there are many peaks above 30% of fog level which is treated as a positive value.

Next (Table 1), some of the most significant points will be deeply analysed to check the veracity of the measurements.

Table 1. Fog level analysis

POINT 2	Fog: 29,67
	False Positive
	City roundabout.
	In the image it appears a white building whose grayscale invalidates the measurement obtaining a value>25 which is considered FOG = TRUE.

POINT 3	Fog: 5,31
	Negative
	Igeldo mountain ascent.
	It is a mountain narrow road, the camera captures the road slopes and the grayscale is greatly low. FOG=FALSE.

POINT 6	Fog: 40,48
	Positive
	Stretch of Igeldo mountain.
	Fog area. The road clears a little bit and the registered level rises (>30). FOG = TRUE.

POINT 11	Fog: 15,55
	Negative
	Stretch of Igeldo mountain.
	Narrow mountain road. The camera captures obstacles at both sides which decreases the grayscale. FOG = FALSE.

POINT 14	Fog: 49,11
	Positive
	Igeldo mountain descend.
	Dense fog area. The level registered by the camera is pretty high (>45). FOG= TRUE.

7 Conclusions

As a major conclusion, it could be said that the system has worked in a positive way. Data have been collected and the server has received all track information which enables the start up of the validation process.

Studying the fog detection algorithm, some conclusions have been derived:

- In local road (inside a city), the presence of obstacles such as buildings could cause invalid measurements. However, this problem could be resolved by analysing the distance while this value has appeared (e.g. the measurement of point 2 was 200 m long).
- In addition, narrow and winding roads nature seems to affect to the obtained signal, which is greatly oscillating. It is necessary to apply a filter.
- After filtering the fog prediction signal some peaks persist, probably due to the obstacles of the road and the camera placement which was focused slightly to the left during this test.

Finally, it is necessary to develop an algorithm for matching the measured fog level with its reliability in a stretch of the road.

References

1. Dirección General de Tráfico. Anuario estadístico de accidentes 2015, pp. 171–173 (2015). http://www.dgt.es/Galerias/seguridad-vial/estadisticas-e-indicadores/publicaciones/anuario-estadistico-de-accidentes/anuario-accidentes-2015.pdf
2. Alhassan, H.M., Ben-Edigbe, J.: Highway capacity prediction in adverse weather. J. Appl. Sci. 11(12), 2193–2199 (2011). doi:10.3923/jas.2011.2193.2199
3. Narasimhan, S.G., Nayar, S.K.: Vision and the atmosphere. Int. J. Comput. Vis. 48(3), 233–254 (2002). doi:10.1023/A:1016328200723
4. Hautière, N., Tarel, J.-P., Lavenant, J., Aubert, D.: Automatic fog detection and estimation of the visibility distance through use of an onboard camera. Mach. Vis. Appl. 17(1), 8–20 (2006). doi:10.1007/s00138-005-0011-1
5. Liu, C., Lu, X., Ji, S., Geng, W.: A fog level detection method based on image HSV color histogram. In: International Conference on IEEE Progress in Informatics and Computing (PIC), pp. 373–377 (2014). doi:10.1109/PIC.2014.6972360

Enhance VEINS Simulator
for Realistic Evaluation Scenarios

Mouna Karoui[1(✉)], Mohamed Kassab[2(✉)],
Hasnaâ Aniss[3(✉)], and Marion Berbineau[1(✉)]

[1] University of Lille Nord de France, IFSTTAR, COSYS,
59650 Villeneuve d'Ascq, France
mounaa.karouii@gmail.com, marion.berbineau@ifsttar.fr
[2] Laboratoire NOCCS, University of Sousse, Sousse, Tunisia
mohamed.kassab@gmail.com
[3] IFSTTAR, COSYS, LIVIC, 78000 Versailles, France
hasnaa.aniss@ifsttar.fr

Abstract. Intelligent transportation systems (ITS) witnessed a great progress through developing new communication applications based on cooperative approach. These applications need a crucial QoS (Quality Of Service) performance and effectiveness. High precision is an eligible condition for ITS safety applications because they are characterized by a real time transmission via cooperative system information. In this paper, we propose a multi-application module for VEINS simulator in order to realize a realistic and dynamic simulation model for performance evaluation of safety and non safety applications on multi-channel operations compared to the single channel operation. Then, we analyze performance of safety and non-safety messages dissemination model for the four EDCA class of the IEEE 1609.4 standard. Our simulations confirm QoS differentiation of IEEE 1609.4 standard and it shows influence of high traffic density on QoS performance.

Keywords: C-ITS · WAVE/IEEE 802.11p · QoS · VEINS

1 Introduction

Cooperative intelligent transportation systems (C-ITS) are today clearly identified as the next step to enhance road safety, improve traffic management and offer various services for road users. To reach these goals, C-ITS defines various applications based on data exchanges between neighbor vehicles and between vehicles and their environment. The importance of these applications varies according to their impact on road safety. They are classified according to this importance into three categories: safety applications, traffic management applications and comfort applications. Data exchanges use Vehicle-to-Vehicle (V2V) and Vehicle-to-Infrastructure (V2I) communications based on wireless technologies. Standardization has been working for several years on the design of wireless communication technologies dedicated to vehicular communication. In particular, the

© Springer International Publishing AG 2017
A. Pirovano et al. (Eds.): Nets4Cars/Nets4Trains/Nets4Aircraft 2017, LNCS 10222, pp. 128–140, 2017.
DOI: 10.1007/978-3-319-56880-5_13

IEEE working groups proposed a protocol stack for these communications: the Wireless Access in Vehicular Environment (WAVE). Several projects have been conducted in C-ITS field in Europe such as GST[1](Global System for Telematics enabling On-line safety services), CVIS[2] (Cooperative Vehicle-Infrastructure Systems), and SAFESPOT[3] were a great opportunity for the design of C-ITS standards and architectures. More recently, research projects like DRIVE C2X[4], SCORE@F[5] and SCOOP@F[6] are focusing on comprehensive, and wide assessment of cooperative systems through field operational tests. For example, the SCOOP@F project aims at deploying cooperative ITS from 2014 onwards. The project will equip 3000 vehicles and 2000 Km of streets, intercity roads and highways in 2016. SCOOP@F involves partners such as local authorities, state services in charge of road management, automotive industries, automotive suppliers, study centers, universities and research centers. The work conducted in these projects are validating the feasibility of C-ITS and their interest for the increase of travel and operation safety, and the improving of travel quality. In addition, they reveal to the international ITS community the need to pursue scalability studies to evaluate the behavior of C-ITS in high scale contexts related to both road congestion situations and highly stressed communication network situations.

In our work, we are interested to offer an evaluation framework, based on simulation tools, for C-ITS applications and communications in the context of real deployments such as the SCOOP@FR project. For that purpose, we consider the open source simulator VEINS (VEhicles In Network Simulation), which is specifically designed for vehicular communications. The features of VEINS are limited and do not enable such kind of experiments. On one hand, VEINS is unable to define a realistic V2I architecture with centralized application servers connected to cars through a set of Road Side Unit (RSU). On the other hand, this framework do not allows the implementation of multi-applications scenarios. We have, therefore, proposed to evolve VEINS modules to allow implementation of realistic scenarios. The purpose of this paper is to present and evaluate these enhancements.

This paper is organized as follow. Section 2 gives an overview of the cooperative ITS architecture, applications and the WAVE protocol stack. Section 3 presents existing works on the subject. Section 4 introduces the VEINS simulation framework. Section 5 details the enhancement proposed to VEINS simulator. Section 6 shows a performance study based on the enhanced simulation framework. Conclusion and future work are presented in Sect. 7.

---

[1] http://cordis.europa.eu/project/rcn/71449_en.html.
[2] http://cordis.europa.eu/project/rcn/79316_en.html.
[3] http://cordis.europa.eu/news/rcn/31165_en.html.
[4] http://cordis.europa.eu/project/rcn/97464_en.html.
[5] http://www.scoref.fr.
[6] http://www.scoop.developpement-durable.gouv.fr.

2   Cooperative ITS and Vehicular Communications

C-ITS are based on vehicular communications where vehicles and network infrastructure are interconnected to each other. Vehicle-to-Vehicle and Vehicle-to-Infrastructure communications use radio transmission to exchange data between applications. With V2I communications, Road Side Units (RSU) are deployed along roads and connected to the communication network infrastructure to handle communications between vehicles and centralized application servers. Cooperative ITS defines three main application categories [1]: safety applications, traffic management applications and comfort applications.

Safety category are related to the enhancement of road safety by the decreasing of road accidents. These applications provide drivers with different services like road hazard and collision warning, cooperative driving assistance and awareness notifications about the road situation.

Traffic management applications are defined to enhance traffic management especially when the road network capacity is exceeded. These applications contribute to improve traffic efficiency by providing services such as dynamic road speed limit management and cooperative optimized navigation.

Comfort applications aim to enhance passenger comfort. Point of interest notifications is an example of comfort application providing multiple services like energy supply station location, maintenance facility, and free parking slots, *etc.*

WAVE/IEEE 802.11p

WAVE (Wireless Access in Vehicular Environment) communication stack is mainly based on the IEEE 802.11p technology and the IEEE 1609.x protocols. WAVE stack enables classic TCP/UDP communications and specific communications as shown in Fig. 1.

The IEEE 802.11p is an adaptation of the well known IEEE 802.11 wireless technology to the WAVE needs. It defines the Medium Access Control (MAC) layer and the physical layer. The IEEE 1609 protocol family includes four standards. The IEEE 1609.1 defines the data and management services offered within the WAVE architecture. The IEEE 1609.2 focus on security services including secure message formats and processing. The IEEE 1609.3 defines network and transport layer services like addressing and routing, and the WAVE Short Message Protocol (WSMP). WSMP allows vehicular applications to transmit Wave Short Messages (WSM) and to control low layer parameters. IEEE 1609.4 standard defines a set of enhancements to IEEE 802.11p MAC in order to implement multi-channel operations.

The IEEE 802.11p divides the 5.9 GHz frequency band into channels: one Control CHannel (CCH) dedicated to safety applications, and several Service CHannels (SCH) used for non-safety data exchanges (e.g. traffic management services and comfort services) [2]. The IEEE 1609.4 multi-channel operations

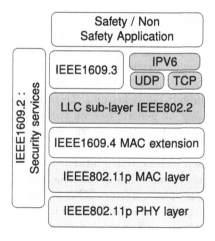

Fig. 1. WAVE/802.11p architecture stack

define the alternative use of the CCH and the SCH during a synchronization interval of 100 ms [3] as illustrated in Fig. 2. This channel access mode is named alternating mode. A continuous mode is also defined and refers to use of a single service channel or the control channel with no channel switching. The medium access defined by the 802.11p is equivalent to he Enhanced Distributed Channel Access (EDCA) defined in by IEEE 802.11e [2]. EDCA inherits from the basic IEEE 802.11 Distributed Coordination Function (DCF) with the use of access categories (AC) to manage QoS. Four access categories (AC) with different priorities are defined. Prioritized access between ACs is defined using specific parameters including maximal and minimal values for the Contention Window (CW) and the Arbitrary Inter-Frame Space (AIFS) timer. The lowest priority is AC0 and the highest one is AC3. Application messages are sorted to the transmission queue associated the application priority [4].

By associating multi-channel operations and Access Categories QoS management, WAVE architecture aims to optimize the use of the radio resources and to favor the applications according to their impact on the reliability of the road.

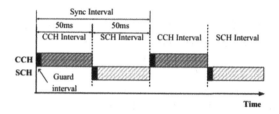

Fig. 2. SCH/CCH interval

3   Related Work

Several research work have studied performances offered by multi-channel operations and QoS management to exchanged data [4–9]. [5] proposed a simulation based performance evaluation of WAVE when channel switching procedures is used. Authors have evaluated the delay and the reception probability of safety applications modeled based on generic beacon traffic exchanged over the CCH (Control CHannel). Results show that alternating mode decrease the performances for beacons.

In [6], authors proposed an adaptive multi-channel assignment based on real-time traffic condition (using congestion measurements). A simulation based performance evaluation was proposed using VEINS for safety and non-safety applications. Generic beacon traffic was considered to implement safety applications. No indication was given about traffic models for non-safety applications. Considering a similar research problematic, [7] proposed an analytic model for WAVE multi-channel operations and a coordination algorithm to enhance multi-channel operations by adjusting the duration of CCH and SCH during a synchronization interval. The impact of proposal was evaluated based on the analytic model and simulation tests. Generic beacon traffics were considered to implement safety and non-safety applications.

In [8], authors proposed a coordination mechanism between RSU transmitting on SCH channels to solve the multi-channel hidden terminal problem. The proposal performances was evaluated based on an analytic model and simulation tests. They evaluated the average throughput on SCH channel while considering a generic traffic (fixed packet size, fixed packet rate) to model the non-safety traffics. In the same context, [9] proposed an Service Channel selection mechanism for non-safety service providers and solve hidden terminal problem in order to enhance SCH utilization. A simulation based performance evaluation was proposed. Safety traffic was implemented based on generic Beacon traffic exchanged over the CCH (Control CHannel) and no indication was given for non-safety traffic.

[4] proposed an analytic model for the performance evaluation of the WAVE QoS management while considering the effects of multi-channel operations. This model was used to evaluate the access delay, packet delivery rate, etc. offered for traffics configured with different Access Categories. Simulation tests were used to prove effectiveness of the proposed model. Data messages are generated considering a Poisson distribution with average rate and fixed message size without differentiating the safety and non-safety traffic. As shown, network simulation is largely used to evaluate the communication performances offered by WAVE architecture. Mainly, these evaluations are implementing generic data traffics without taking into account the specifications of the applications in their models. This type of simulation enables the global evaluation of communication technology performances. However, it does not offer a clear view of performances perceived by the different types of application that can be defined by ITS.

4   VEhicles in Network Simulation (VEINS)

VEINS[7] is an open source simulation framework for vehicular communications. It is based on the network simulator OMNET++ and the traffic road simulation environment SUMO, as illustrated in Fig. 3.

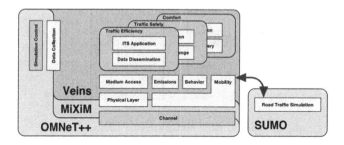

Fig. 3. Modular structure of VEINS

OMNET++ is an extensible network simulation environment programmed with the C++ language. It offers the NED (NEtwork Description) as a description language that enables the assembly of communication components into network entities and network entities into network typologies.

VEINS makes use of the OMNET++ simulation kernel for discrete-event simulation of network functions and SUMO for the simulation of vehicle mobility. The simulation execution is then based on the running of OMNET++ and SUMO simulators in parallel. The connection between the two simulators is ensured by TCP socket. The protocol for this communication is named Traffic Interface Control (TraCI) [10]. VEINS implements the whole WAVE protocol stack using C++ and NED languages. The modular implementation of protocols based on the object-oriented programming language C++ makes this tool flexible and easy to extend [11]. In the following we are presenting the implementation of the WAVE architecture proposed by VEINS.

VEINS offers two types of network entities to implement vehicular communication scenarios: Cars and Road Side Unit (RSU). As shown in Fig. 4, VEINS RSU consists of three main components:

- *Network Interface Card (NIC)*: implements the IEEE 802.11p technology including the MAC and PHY layers. It is composed of two simple NED modules: *MAC1609.4* and *PHY802.11p* connected to each others based NED gates.
- *Mobility*: configures the RSU position.
- *Application*: implements an application level that generates WSMP data that can simulate V2I traffic sent form an RSU to cars. The equivalent structure is proposed for the Car entity.

---

[7] http://veins.car2x.org/.

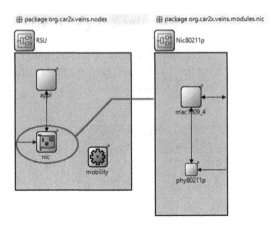

Fig. 4. RSU structure in VEINS

MAC1609.4 and PHY802.11p NED components include a set of C ++ classes that implement the functions of PHY and MAC layers. This include particularly the multi-channel operations and the EDCA medium access and QoS management.

The *Application* NED component implements a WSMP based application layer. The *BaseWAVEApplLayer* class implements the transmission and reception of WAVE Short Message (WSM), inheriting form the classes *BaseApplLayer* and *BaseLayer*, as shown in blue in Fig. 6. It is important to notice here that based on *Application* NED component, we can implement only one application in each network entity (car and/or RSU). This is one main limit of VEINS. In addition, RSU entities are defined as a standalone entities. They integrate an *Application* component to act as a infrastructure traffic generator and they can not be connected to a centralized network. Thus, it is not possible to set up a network architecture offering a set of RSUs federated through a wired network and connected to centralized servers.

5   Enhanced Simulation Module

Choosing VEINS for our V2X simulations is a logical decision because it is favorable for academic research. As discussed before, it presents a well-established model for WAVE architecture. Furthermore, it presents flow and traffic models typically based on physical equations developed to provide accident-free and optimal traffic spreading. Thus, it helps to reproduce the realistic microscopic V2X interactions observed when evaluating safety and non-safety applications.

Our research aims to simulate realistic scenarios in the context actual C-ITS deployments. However, VEINS features are limited as explained in Sect. 4. We propose a set of modifications to VEINS modules to be able to simulate:

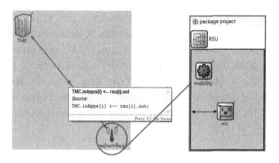

Fig. 5. RSU proposed model

- Realistic network architecture for V2I communication including centralized network with servers and RSUs deployed along roads.
- multi-application context with different applications share V2V and V2I communications.

The first step is to extract *Application* NED component from RSU entity, and to override it in the Traffic Manager Control (TMC) entity. Figure 5 shows our proposed RSU model composed of *NIC* and *mobility* components. It has input and output NED gates to connect it to the TMC entity. The latter includes *Application* NED component that implements a new C++ Class *TMCApps* that Inherits from *BaseWAVEApplLayer* class. *TMCApps* is able to implement independently a set of applications with specific traffic behaviors.

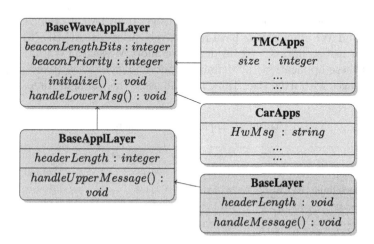

Fig. 6.   Class   diagram   Blue: VEINS base classes   Red: Added classes (Color figure online)

In addition, the TMC entity implements an input connector table that is dynamically allocated according to RSU number. Connection between TMC and RSU is ensured by NED gates of both RSU and TMC modules shown in Fig. 6.

In addition, we have modified[8] *Application* component of the Car entity to implement a new C++ class *CarApps*. This new class is able to implement independently a set of applications with specific traffic behaviors for the car in the same way as *TMCApps* class. New classes are drawn in red in Fig. 6.

6   Performance Evaluation

We present in this section simulation tests to validate the enhancement we proposed to the VEINS simulation framework. We select a set of ITS applications modeling the application categories presented in Sect. 2.

Hazard warning (HW) is an event-driven safety application. It defines the broadcast of safety message by a vehicle when it notices a hazard through the road. Messages are broadcast to one-hop neighbor vehicles. If an RSU gets the message it forwards it to the TMC. The later then broadcasts it to vehicles in a more large area through RSUs. HW application has the highest IEEE 802.11p priority AC-VO (3).

Dynamic speed limit (DSL) is a traffic management application. It defines the broadcast of speed limit messages from TMC to vehicles through RSUs. The IEEE 802.11p priority attributed to DSL application is AC-VI (2).

Point of interest (PI) and weather information (WI) are comfort applications. They define the broadcast of information messages from TMC to vehicles through RSUs. PI and WI applications have respectively priorities AC-BE (0) and AC-BK (1). For test scenarios, we consider Wave Short Messages (WSMs). We have simplified these applications by defining a periodic generation (fixed period) of WSM messages with fixed size. Table 1 summarizes this configuration.

Table 1. Applications parameters

ITS services	Priorities	Message length	Inter-Message time	Communication
Hazard warning	AC-VO (3)	1282 bytes	95 ms	V2I and V2V
Dynamic speed limit	AC-VI (2)	1282 bytes	95 ms	I2V
Point of interest	AC-BE (0)	1282 bytes	95 ms	I2V
Weather information	AC-BK (1)	1282 bytes	95 ms	I2V

We consider a simple network architecture with two RSUs covering a 2500 m 2-lanes highway. Figure 7 shows the considered network topology. We vary the

---

[8] https://github.com/Mounakaroui/AppsModuleFor_VEINS_Simulator.

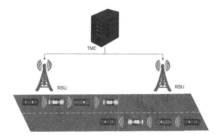

Fig. 7. Network topology

number of vehicles from 20 to 100. Each vehicle is equipped with an IEEE 802.11p network interface card on which the HW application is implemented. Vehicles are moving according to a maximal speed of 12.5 m/s. Table 2 summarizes this configuration.

Table 2. Scenario parameters

Hightway length	2500 m
Number of RSU	2
RSU transmission range	512 m
Number of vehicles	[20–100]
Max vehicle Speed	12.5 m/s
Simulation Time	400 s

To evaluate the performances offered by applications, we consider two key performance indicators:

– *End-to-End Delay (E2E Delay)*: refers to the average time needed by messages of an application to reach the destination.
– *Throughput*: refers to the average of successfully received data per second

We consider successively the continuous and alternating modes defined by the WAVE. In the first mode, all messages are exchanged, regardless their applications, on the CCH channel. In the second mode, HW application messages are exchanged on the CCH channel and DSL, PI and WI applications messages are exchanged on an SCH channel. We run the simulation scenario in each mode while varying the number of vehicles.

Figures 8 and 9 show the E2E Delay for the applications with respectively the alternating and continuous modes. For data exchanged on the SCH channel (alternating mode), E2E Delay is more important for all applications compared to continuous mode. This is an expected result, as in alternating mode wireless access for applications is available alternatively (50 ms for each channel).

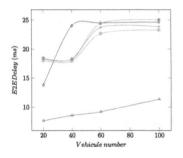

Fig. 8. E2E Delay in alternating mode

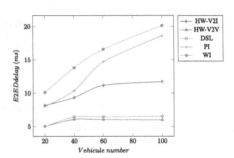

Fig. 9. E2E Delay in continuous mode

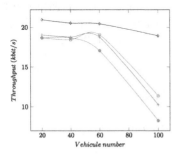

Fig. 10. Throughput in alternating mode

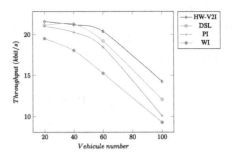

Fig. 11. Throughput in continuous mode

In the both modes, hazard warning V2V has the lowest E2E Delay and Weather Information the highest one. This is also an expected result given the priority assignment (the highest priority for HW and the lowest for WI). We have to notice that for HW V2I, delays are considerably greater than the ones obtained for HW V2V, which is also expected. With HW V2I, messages are sent by a sending vehicle to the TMC, through an RSU, and then forwarded to a receiver vehicle. However, being favored by priorities, even with the V2I exchange HW obtains better performances than DSL, WI and PI applications as shown in Fig. 9.

Figures 10 and 11 present the average throughput experienced by applications with respectively the alternating and the continuous modes. For this performance indicator, we consider only V2I exchanges for the HW application given the difficulty to isolate the messages generated by one vehicles for V2V exchanges. The first observation is that the results obtained are in accordance with the priorities assigned to the applications as V2I exchanges of HW application have the highest average throughput in the two modes. However, alternating access offers the best throughput in comparison with continuous mode for HW application. This is expected as with alternating mode HW application is the only application to use the channel while in continuous mode it shares the channel with the other applications.

For the DSL, PI and WI applications we observe better performance with continuous mode. This result is logical as in alternate mode, these applications share the bandwidth with half time access while in the continuous mode they share the access continuously over time (with the HW application).

7   Conclusion and Future Work

Network simulation is an essential tool for research related to cooperative ITS and vehicular communications. Indeed, simulation frameworks offer a way to evaluate performances of ITS applications within contexts hardly achievable in real work such as actual deployments and scalability tests. However, such kind of evaluations requires simulation tools able to implement network architectures and applications close to reality. In this work, we have proposed a set of enhancements to VEINS simulation framework to be able to implement realistic network architectures and multi-application contexts. We have realized a set of simulation scenarios to evaluate the performances offered to cooperative applications including a safety application, a traffic management application and two comfort applications. The obtained results have validated our simulation module regarding specially QoS differentiation and alternating mode use. In addition, we showed the ability of proposed simulation module to implement realistic scenarios. In our future work, we target to use this enhancement to evaluate more complex actual deployments such as urban contexts while considering a more realistic application load.

Acknowledgement. This work was supported by the SCOOF@FR project.

References

1. ITS, T.C.: Intelligent transport systems (its); vehicular communications; basic set of applications; definitions. Technical report 102 638 V1.1.1, ETSI (2009)
2. IEEE: Part 11: Wireless LAN medium access control (MAC) and physical layer (PHY) specifications amendment 6: Wireless access in vehicular environments, pp. 1–51, July 2010
3. IEEE: Standard for wireless access in vehicular environments (wave) - multi-channel operation, pp. 1–206, March 2016
4. Zhou, P., Liu, Y., Wang, J., Deng, W., Oh, H.: Performance analysis of prioritized broadcast service in WAVE/IEEE 802.11p. Computer Networks (2016)
5. van Eenennaam, M., vande Venis, A., Karagiannis, G.: Impact of IEEE 1609.4 channel switching on the IEEE 802.11p beaconing performance. In: Wireless Days (WD), 2012 IFIP, pp. 1–8. IEEE (2012)
6. Chantaraskul, S., Chaitien, K., Nirapai, A., Tanwongvarl, C.: Safety communication based adaptive multi-channel assignment for vanets. In: Wireless Personal Communications, pp. 1–16 (2015)
7. Xiong, K., Chen, X., Rao, L., Liu, X., Yao, Y.: Solving the performance puzzle of DSRC multi-channel operations. In: 2015 IEEE International Conference on Communications (ICC), pp. 3843–3848. IEEE (2015)

8. Li, X., Hu, B.J., Chen, H., Andrieux, G., Wang, Y., Wei, Z.H.: An RSU-coordinated synchronous multi-channel MAC scheme for vehicular ad hoc networks. IEEE Access **3**, 2794–2802 (2015)

9. Lee, D., Ahmed, S.H., Kim, D., Copeland, J., Chang, Y.: An efficient SCH utilization scheme for IEEE 1609.4 multi-channel environments in vanets. In: 2016 IEEE International Conference on Communications (ICC), pp. 1–6. IEEE (2016)

10. Krajzewicz, D., Erdmann, J., Behrisch, M., Bieker, L.: Recent development and applications of sumo-simulation of urban mobility. Int. J. Adv. Syst. Meas. **5**(3&4) (2012)

11. Kim, O.T.T., Nguyen, V., Hong, C.S.: Which network simulation tool is better for simulating vehicular ad-hoc network? Corea Ciencias de la Información Sociedad de la **41**(2014), 930–932 (2014)

Cognitive Radio for Real-Time Wireless Communications

Raul Torrego, Ander Etxabe, Pedro M. Rodriguez, Cristina Cruces,
Aitor Arriola, and Iñaki Val[✉]

Information and Communication Technologies, IK4-IKERLAN,
Arrasate-Mondragon, Spain
{rtorrego, aetxabe, pmrodriguez, ccruces,
aarriola, ival}@ikerlan.es

This work presents a jamming-resistant and deterministic wireless communication system, which is intended to be used in industrial communications. These kind of applications require data communication to be bounded in the time and reliability domains, no matter which is the harshness of the environment or the presence of malicious interferences. In harsh propagation environments, communication systems suffer from severe signal degradation, including delay spread, deep fading and Doppler spread. Besides, they must also deal with other system's interference and jammer attacks.

Unfortunately, traditional wireless communication systems are not able to overcome all these difficulties and, at the same time, fulfill with the aforementioned requirements. As a consequence, it is necessary to deploy new wireless communication systems like the one presented in this work, based on cognitive radio technology. The proposed wireless communication system, shown in Fig. 1, is based on a custom Orthogonal Frequency Division Multiplexing (OFDM) modem design which has been implemented on the programmable logic of a Xilinx Zynq Field Programmable Gate Array (FPGA). The modem is fully customizable, in case it is needed to add new features, and it is similar to the IEEE 802.11a/g physical layer standard. On top of this modem, a deterministic, real-time and cognitive Medium Access Control (MAC) layer has been implemented and evaluated. Based on a Time Division Multiple Access (TDMA) MAC, which ensures deterministic communications in the absence of interference, cognitive capabilities have been added. Unlike traditional cognitive radios, which are used in order to enhance spectrum utilization, the presented wireless communication system is able to detect interference (malicious or coming from other wireless communication systems) and switch the communication to an unoccupied and safe frequency band.

A. Pirovano et al. (Eds.): Nets4Cars/Nets4Trains/Nets4Aircraft 2017, LNCS 10222, pp. 141–142, 2017.
DOI: 10.1007/978-3-319-56880-5

Fig. 1. Detail of the test setup: OFDM modem and jammer.

A test setup has been prepared with the communication system configured with a frame length of 3.85 ms and a data lifetime of 30 ms. Besides, a jammer generating interferences has been added. In a scenario in which only the frequency the communication system is working is interfered, a single frequency hop is forced and a recovery time bounded between 8.5 and 12.5 ms is achieved. If both, the frequency in which the communication system is working and the one into the first hop is performed are interfered, thus forcing two frequency hops, the achieved recovery time is bounded between 20 and 23.7 ms. In both scenarios the 30 ms data lifetime is fulfilled.

Author Index

Printed in the United States
By Bookmasters